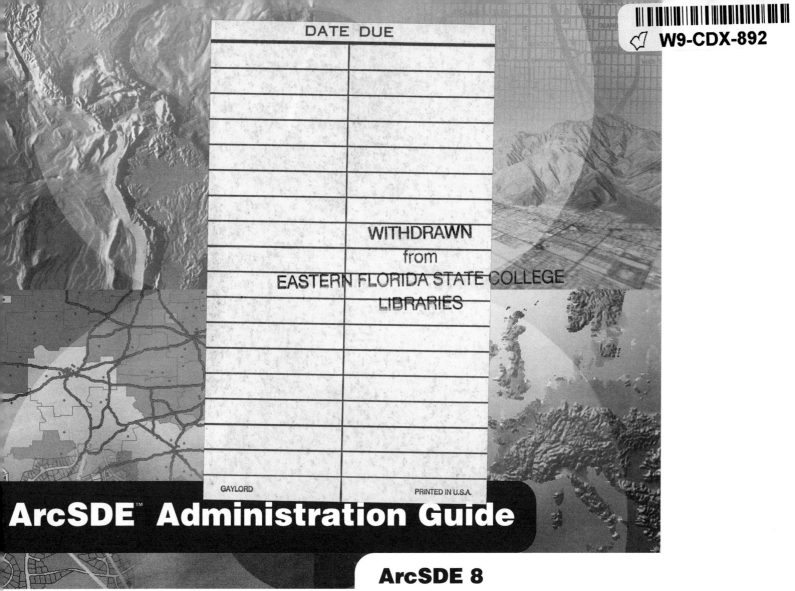

W9-CDX-892

ArcSDE™ Administration Guide

ArcSDE 8

Mark Harris and Jillian Clark

Contents

Introducing the ArcSDE service

This chapter introduces the key components of the ArcSDE™ service and provides an overview of the underlying service configuration. Subsequent chapters discuss in more detail the creation, configuration, and management of the ArcSDE service. The appendices in this book contain detailed descriptions of the ArcSDE home directory, the data dictionary, table definitions, a full listing of the ArcSDE commands, and the ArcSDE initialization parameters.

What is an ArcSDE service?

An ArcSDE service conveys spatial data between geographic information system (GIS) applications and a database. The database may be any one of the supported relational database management systems (RDBMSs) such as Oracle®, SQL Server™, Informix®, Sybase®, or DB2®. The database could also be a registered collection of ArcInfo™ coverages, or shapefiles. The applications that can connect to and access spatial data from an ArcSDE service include ArcInfo, ArcView® GIS, MapObjects®, ArcIMS™, and ArcSDE CAD Client, as well as custom-built applications created by either you or an ESRI business partner.

The ArcSDE service

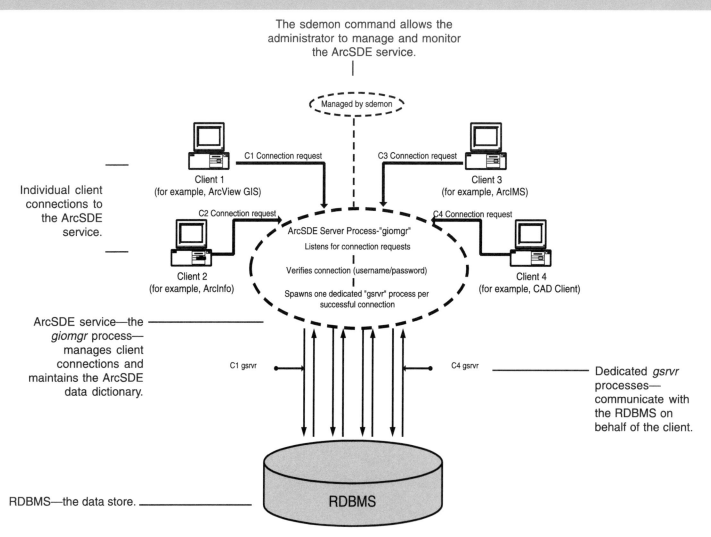

The sdemon command allows the administrator to manage and monitor the ArcSDE service.

Managed by sdemon

Individual client connections to the ArcSDE service.

C1 Connection request

Client 1
(for example, ArcView GIS)

C3 Connection request

Client 3
(for example, ArcIMS)

C2 Connection request

Client 2
(for example, ArcInfo)

ArcSDE Server Process-"giomgr"

Listens for connection requests

Verifies connection (username/password)

Spawns one dedicated "gsrvr" process per successful connection

C4 Connection request

Client 4
(for example, CAD Client)

ArcSDE service—the *giomgr* process—manages client connections and maintains the ArcSDE data dictionary.

C1 gsrvr

C4 gsrvr

Dedicated *gsrvr* processes—communicate with the RDBMS on behalf of the client.

RDBMS—the data store.

RDBMS

Properties of an ArcSDE service

The ArcSDE service has a number of defining properties; these are introduced in the following sections.

The home directory

Each ArcSDE service has its own home directory, which is defined by the system variable, SDEHOME. The home directory contains the ArcSDE binary executable files, dynamic shared libraries, configuration files, and internationalization code pages. The contents of the ArcSDE home directory are listed in 'Appendix A: ArcSDE home directory'.

The ArcSDE server monitor—the giomgr process

Each ArcSDE service has one giomgr process. This process listens for user application connection requests, spawns gsrvr processes, cleans up disconnected user processes, and also maintains the ArcSDE data dictionary.

The gsrvr process

The giomgr process spawns a gsrvr process for each application connected to the ArcSDE service. The gsrvr process is dedicated to a single-user application connection. It communicates with the database on behalf of the connected application. The gsrvr process responds to the application's query and edit requests to the database.

The TCP/IP service name and port number

The ArcSDE service, through the giomgr process, listens for application connection requests on a dedicated TCP/IP service name and port number. The gsrvr process, in turn, communicates with the application on the same TCP/IP service and port number. All communication between the applications and the ArcSDE service take place using the TCP/IP service name and port number.

The database

Each ArcSDE service connects to its own database. A database can have only one ArcSDE service connected to it. Multiple connections are prevented through a locating mechanism. Once an ArcSDE service has started and the connection to the database has been established, the service locks the database. If any attempt is made to start a second ArcSDE service and connect it to the same database, an error results and the second ArcSDE service automatically shuts down.

The configuration files

The ArcSDE service can be configured to control the number of application connections as well as the operating system resources each connection may obtain. It can also be configured to optimize the data flow between the connected applications and the database.

About this book

If it is your task to create and maintain an ArcSDE service, then you should read this book. This book discusses the ArcSDE service—how to create the service as well as how to manage and monitor its usage.

What's not covered in this book

The focus of this book is not the creation or administration of an RDBMS. This is a separate topic that is covered briefly in the *ArcSDE Configuration and Tuning Guide for <RDBMS>* PDF file, config_tuning_guide_<rdbms>.pdf, located in the documentation folder on the ArcSDE CD.

Creating ArcSDE services

2

When you install ArcSDE, the default ArcSDE service is created. The directory into which the ArcSDE software and ancillary directories are copied is called the home directory, or SDEHOME, of the default ArcSDE service. For a complete list of the directories and files copied to the ArcSDE home directory, refer to 'Appendix A: ArcSDE home directory'.

Before an ArcSDE service can be started, four important prerequisites should be considered:

- The ArcSDE software has been installed correctly, and the default home directory (SDEHOME) has been established. Any installation errors will be reported to the <SDEHOME>\SDE80ORA.LOG file.

- ArcSDE products, other than ArcSDE for Coverages, require the presence of an RDBMS database.

- An ArcSDE user account must exist in the RDBMS with enough free space available to store the ArcSDE data dictionary.

- A unique TCP/IP service name and port number must be available.

The ArcSDE home directory

The ArcSDE home directory, also known by the system variable that stores its location (either %SDEHOME% on Windows NT or $SDEHOME on UNIX), contains all of the executable files and dynamic libraries required to run an ArcSDE service. This directory structure is automatically set up during the installation process. Each independent ArcSDE service requires its own home directory.

If the host computer on which ArcSDE is installed is going to run a single ArcSDE service, all that is required is to edit the configuration files. However, if the host computer is going to support multiple ArcSDE services, you must create additional home directories and copy the directories found under the default home directory into the new home directories using the operating system copy command.

The ArcSDE service's configuration files must then be updated to reflect the unique properties of the new service. Many ArcSDE services can run on a single computer, with each service requiring its own home directory, database, TCP/IP service name and port number, and an SdeServer license. The hardware platform must have sufficient resources available to support the processes of the ArcSDE software and the RDBMS.

The RDBMS database

ArcSDE stores data in an RDBMS database. This database must exist before the ArcSDE service can be created. Consult your RDBMS documentation for guidance on creating an RDBMS database. You should also review the basic advice provided in the *ArcSDE Configuration and Tuning Guide for <RDBMS>,* which is located in the documents directory of the CD–ROM installation media and in the ArcSDE home directory (SDEHOME).

SQL Server, Informix, Sybase, and DB2 support servers that may contain one or more databases, although be aware that RDBMS vendors vary in their definition of a database. An ArcSDE service can only connect to one database server and to one database.

Configuration parameters that control the manner in which an ArcSDE service connects to a database may be stored in the dbinit.sde file. This file is located in the %SDEHOME%\etc directory on Windows NT and in the $SDEHOME/etc directory on UNIX. This avoids the need to rely on environment variables set when the user logs in. The dbinit.sde file is discussed in detail in Chapter 3, 'Configuring ArcSDE services'.

For optimum performance, the database and the ArcSDE service should coexist on the same host. However, it is possible for ArcSDE to connect to a database hosted on a remote machine. For more information on establishing a remote connection to an ArcSDE service, please refer to *ArcSDE Configuration and Tuning Guide for <RDBMS>.*

The ArcSDE RDBMS administration account

ArcSDE service requires the creation of an ArcSDE RDBMS administration account. The installation process gave you the opportunity to create this user and the necessary RDBMS tablespace. If this step was bypassed during the installation, it must be completed before the ArcSDE service can be started up.

The procedure for creating the ArcSDE RDBMS administration account differs for each ArcSDE product. For information on how to create this user, please refer to *install_guide.pdf* in the documentation directory under the home directory (SDEHOME) for your particular ArcSDE installation.

Under this user account, ArcSDE stores its data dictionary tables. The data dictionary tables require approximately 40 MB of free space, so it is important that the ArcSDE RDBMS user has access to sufficient resources to accommodate this.

The ArcSDE service on UNIX and Windows NT

Each ArcSDE service listens for user connections on a dedicated TCP/IP service name and port number through the giomgr process.

On UNIX systems, edit the $SDEHOME/etc/services.sde file and the /etc/services file to include the name of the ArcSDE service.

On Windows NT systems, the ArcSDE service is created as a Windows NT service. The service name is stored in the registry under HKEY_LOCAL_MACHINE\ SOFTWARE\ESRI\ArcInfo\ ArcSde\8.0\Arcsde for <product>\<service name>. ▶

Tip

Port number
Although it is not used at this stage, the port number in the SDEHOME/etc/services.sde file is included to remind the ArcSDE administrator that the service name is assigned to the 5151/TCP port in the operating system services file.

Registering an ArcSDE service on UNIX

1. Edit the $SDEHOME/etc/services.sde file.

2. Add the same service name and port number to the operating system /etc/services file.

```
#
# ESRI ArcSDE service name and port number
#
esri_sde          5151/tcp ————————————①
```
$SDEHOME/etc/services.sde file

```
.
.
.
nfsd      2049/udp  # NFS server daemon (clts)
nfsd      2049/tcp  # NFS server daemon (cots)
lockd     4045/udp  # NFS lock daemon/manager
lockd     4045/tcp
esri_sde  5151/tcp  # ArcSDE 8 service ————————②
dtspc     6112/tcp  # CDE subprocess control
fs        7100/tcp  # Font server
.
.
```
Operating system /etc/services file

The installation program automatically enters the service name and port number for the default ArcSDE service in both the registry and the Windows NT services file, C:\winnt\system32\drivers\etc\services.

The installation program also creates the Windows NT service, setting it to automatic—that is, it will automatically start up when the server host is rebooted.

Like all Windows NT services, the ArcSDE service is started and stopped from the Windows NT services menu.

While it is possible to start the ArcSDE service with the sdemon command from MS–DOS®, it is not recommended. However, because error messages are printed directly to the MS–DOS command window instead of the event log, using sdemon to start the service can be useful when trying to diagnose a startup problem. Unlike the Windows NT service, the sdemon command reads the service name from %SDEHOME%\etc\services.sde file. Edit this file to ensure that it contains the correct information before using sdemon.

Verifying an ArcSDE service on Windows NT

1. Open the Control Panel and double-click Services.

2. Verify the ArcSDE service has been started.

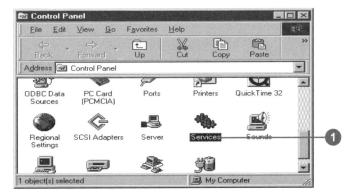

Monitoring the ArcSDE service

1. Use the sdemon command at the Windows® MS–DOS command prompt to trap ArcSDE service error messages.

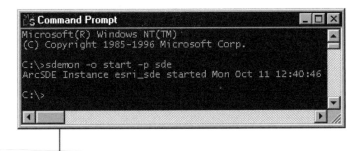

Accessing an ArcSDE service through a firewall

To provide access to an ArcSDE service inside a system security *firewall,* the host computer on which the ArcSDE service is installed should be listed in your domain name server (DNS) database. The domain name server must be registered with your Internet Service Provider (ISP) or directly with InterNIC (now called Network Solutions), the organization that registers Internet domain names.

Your DNS resolves the IP address of your computer to the name, or Unique Resource Locator (URL), you wish to make accessible to the Internet. In most cases, you will have more machines within your local network than you will have Internet IP addresses for. In this case, you would maintain your own set of internal IP addresses known only to your Local Area Network (LAN). Your firewall, or proxy server software, will translate your internal IP addresses to Internet IP addresses when you access computers outside your LAN.

Since ArcSDE services listen for connections on a TCP/IP port number that corresponds to your ArcSDE service name, you must also add the TCP/IP port number to the server name when connecting to it. You can specify an ArcSDE server name in two ways. You can either use the DNS name if it is available, or you can connect to it directly using its Internet IP address.

For example, our domain name esri.com has been registered with InterNIC, and we identified our DNS as IP address 198.102.62.1. Our DNS has the IP address for the ArcSDE server Toshi in its DNS database. The internal IP address for Toshi is 46.1.2.324, which is translated to the IP address 198.102.62.5 when Toshi sends and receives information through the firewall. The ArcSDE service running on Toshi is listening for connections on the service name esri_sde3, which corresponds to TCP/IP port number 5165. So if you wish to connect to that particular ArcSDE service, you must specify either the server name "toshi.esri.com:5165" or identify Toshi by its IP address "198.102.62.5:5165". In both cases you must also include the service port number, 5165.

If you cannot connect to an ArcSDE service through a firewall, test the accessibility of the remote ArcSDE server with your Internet browser by specifying either the server name and TCP/IP port number or the IP address and TCP/IP port number as the URL.

The correct syntax is:

```
<server name>:<port number>
<IP address>:<port number>
```

Configuring ArcSDE services

3

ArcSDE conveys spatial data between an RDBMS and applications. Configuring an ArcSDE service focuses on maximizing data transfer between the server and the client with limited shared resources. The requirements of the application, the number of users, and the amount of data requested influence the configuration of the ArcSDE service.

The ArcSDE service can be configured by modifying the parameters in the configuration files found under the SDEHOME\etc directory. The four configuration files are services.sde, dbinit.sde, giomgr.def, and dbtune.sde.

The services.sde file

Each ArcSDE service communicates with the RDBMS and the applications through a TCP/IP port. TCP/IP ports are defined by name in the operating system's services file.

The SDEHOME\etc\services.sde file contains the service name, the unique TCP/IP port number on which the ArcSDE service accepts connection requests. This port number is also assigned to each user or gsrvr process that the ArcSDE service initiates. The port number listed in the services.sde file is not used but is included by convention as a reminder of the port number assigned to the service name in the operating system's services file.

The default esri_sde service name and 5151 TCP/IP port number are registered with the Information Sciences Institute, Internet Assigned Numbers Authority.

The default services.sde file created during the installation process will contain the following:

```
#
# ESRI ArcSDE Remote Protocol
#
esri_sde              5151/tcp
```

To change the default ArcSDE service name, simply edit the file and restart the service.

When the ArcSDE service is started with the sdemon command, the service searches the system services file for a service name that matches the service name in the services.sde file.

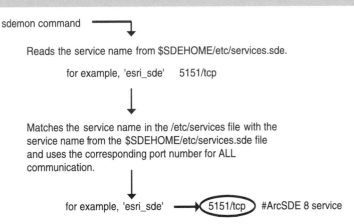

Mapping the SDEHOME/etc/services.sde entries to the system services file entries

When a match is found, ArcSDE starts the giomgr process. It listens on the TCP/IP port number assigned to the service name for user connection requests.

If a match is not found, ArcSDE returns the following error on UNIX systems:

```
$ sdemon -o start
Please enter the SDE DBA password: *****
This instance's service name esri_sde not found
in system services file.
```

To diagnose startup problems on a Windows NT platform, examine the event log. For more information, see Chapter 6, 'Troubleshooting the ArcSDE service'.

Multiple ArcSDE services running on the same host require unique service names and port numbers. If you intend to create another ArcSDE service on the same host, you must edit one of the services.sde files and amend the service name and port number accordingly. You must also update the system services file to include the new ArcSDE service.

The services.sde file in each SDEHOME\etc directory should contain only one service name. If you add more than one service name to this file, ArcSDE uses the first one it encounters and ignores the rest.

The operating system services file contains many service names. At least one of them must match your ArcSDE service name in the services.sde file. Enter the service name into the operating system services file on the ArcSDE server and client machines.

Here is an example from an operating system services file that contains two ArcSDE services:

```
esri_sde 5151/tcp  sde   # ArcSDE def instance
                         # iomgr port.
esri_sde2 5161/tcp  sde2 # ArcSDE instance
                         # 2 iomgr port.
```

This defines two service names: esri_sde and esri_sde2.

On UNIX systems, you can use the NIS services file if you are running NIS to avoid unnecessary duplication of effort when updating the client and server local system services files.

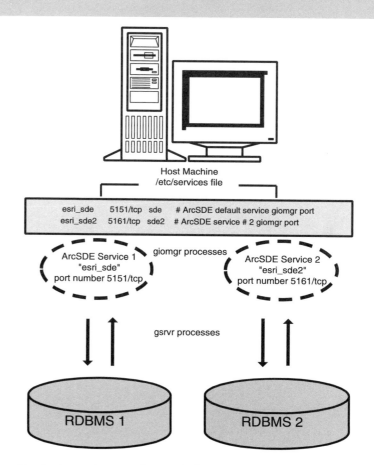

One host computer supporting two ArcSDE services

Operating system services files

The services file on a Windows NT platform is located under the winnt\system32\drivers\etc directory. Use an editor such as Notepad that does not embed format characters to edit the Windows NT services file.

The services file for UNIX systems is located at /etc/services.

Some UNIX systems direct applications to search the NIS services file rather than the host's services file. In this case, you must force a search of the local services file.

Forcing a search of local services on HP-UX®

1. Copy the nsswitch.conf file from the /usr/newconfig/etc directory to the /etc directory.

2. Edit the file and change the line 'services: nis files' to 'services: files nis'.

Forcing a search of the local services on IBM® AIX®

1. In the /etc directory, create the file netsvc.conf.

2. Add the line "services=local.nis".

```
# /etc/nsswitch.conf:

#This file uses NIS (YP) in conjunction with
# files.

# "hosts:" and "services:" in this file are used
# only if the /etc/netconfig file has a "-" for
# nametoaddr_libs of "inet" transports.

# the following two lines obviate the "+" entry
# in /etc/passwd and /etc/group.

passwd:         files nis
group:          files nis
# consult /etc "files" only if nis is down.
hosts:          files nis dns
networks:       nis [NOTFOUND=return] files
protocols:      nis [NOTFOUND=return] files
rpc:            nis [NOTFOUND=return] files
ethers:         nis [NOTFOUND=return] files
netmasks:       nis [NOTFOUND=return] files
bootparams:     nis [NOTFOUND=return] files
publickey:      nis [NOTFOUND=return] files
netgroup:       nis
automount:      files nis
aliases:        files nis
# for efficient getservbyname() avoid nis
services:       files nis ————————————————————— ➋
sendmailvars:   files
```

The ArcSDE service name on Windows NT

On Windows NT systems, the services.sde file is only accessed when the ArcSDE service is started with the sdemon command. When the service is started from the services menu, the service name is read from the system registry.

To change the service name in the Windows NT registry, use the sdeservice administration command.

See Also

For more information about the sdeservice command, see 'Appendix D: ArcSDE command references'.

1. Shut down the ArcSDE service from the Windows NT service menu by selecting Stop.

2. Remove the old service name using the sdeservice command with the delete option.

3. Create the new service name with the sdeservice -o create option.

4. Restart the ArcSDE service from the service menu. Notice the service name has changed.

❷ `sdeservice -o delete -i esri_sde`

❸ `sdeservice -o create  -p password -l 27005@bongo -d ORACLE8I,bruno -i arcsde8`

ArcSDE RDBMS system environment variables

The ArcSDE service uses system environment variables in the SDEHOME\etc\dbinit.sde file to establish the RDBMS server that it connects to and to limit the messages written to the sde.errlog file. If these system environment variables are not set in the dbinit.sde file, the ArcSDE service uses the variables set within the user's system environment. If the variables are not set in either the dbinit.sde file or the current user environment, default ArcSDE settings are used.

The system environment variables that control the ArcSDE services connection to an RDBMS depend on each individual RDBMS.

Setting RDBMS-specific variables

Informix

SDE_ADMINDB—The ODBC data source that connects to the ArcSDE database

SDE_USERDB—The ODBC data source that connects to the default database

Oracle

ORACLE_HOME—The full path to the Oracle installation

ORACLE_SID—The Oracle instance the ArcSDE service will connect to

or

TWO_TASK—The Oracle service to connect to (UNIX)

LOCAL—The Oracle service to connect to (Windows NT)

Sybase

SYBASE—The full path to the Sybase installation.

DSQUERY—The Sybase server the ArcSDE service will connect to.

DB2

set SDE_DATABASE=sde

ArcSDE system environment variables

These environment variables control messages written to the screen at startup and to the sde.errlog file during ArcSDE run time.

SDEDBECHO echoes the contents of the dbinit.sde file during startup. For ArcSDE services started locally on a UNIX system, the output of SDEDBECHO is written to the screen. The SDEDBECHO output for an ArcSDE service started on a remote UNIX ArcSDE service is written to its sde.errlog file.

SDEVERBOSE reports internal messaging to the screen upon startup and writes gsrvr process startup and shutdown messages to sde.errlog.

SDETMP allows you to set the temp directory for the servers using this variable, but it will only be checked if there is no TEMP keyword in the giomgr.defs file.

The dbinit.sde file format

The dbinit.sde file consists of comments and commands. Comments are any lines preceded by the pound sign "#". For example:

```
# This is the system environment for ArcSDE
service esri_sde
```

The commands in the dbinit.sde file accept two keywords: set and unset. The set command enables the system variable and assigns it the value following the equals sign. The syntax of the set command is:

```
set <variable>=<value>
```

In this example, the SDEDBECHO variable is set to true, which echoes the variables set in the dbinit.sde file when the ArcSDE service is started.

```
set SDEDBECHO TRUE
```

The unset command disables the system variable. It is useful because it ensures that an undesired variable set in the login environment is not set when ArcSDE starts. The syntax of the unset command is:

```
unset <variable>
```

The following example of the unset command ensures that the Oracle TWO_TASK variable is not set:

```
unset TWO_TASK
```

Displaying ArcSDE system environment variables

To display the environment variables for an ArcSDE service, use:

```
$ sdemon -o info -I vars
```

A list of environment variables is returned in the format <variable>=<value>.

Part of the list will look something like this on a UNIX platform:

```
SDEHOME=/cymru1/sde80
ESRI_LICENSE_FILE=27005@ynysmon
```

The list will look something like this on a Windows NT platform:

```
SDEHOME=C:\ProgramFiles\ESRI\ArcInfo\arcsde\sdeexe80
ESRI_LICENSE_FILE=27005@ynysmon
```

The variables in either list are a combination of those found in the login system environment file (.cshrc or .profile file on UNIX systems and the environment tab of the Windows NT control panel's system menu) and the dbinit.sde. The variables set in the dbinit.sde file always override the system environment files settings.

Adjusting ArcSDE service initialization parameters

The ArcSDE service initialization parameters set in the SDEHOME\etc\giomgr.defs file affect such things as the number of connections that can be made to the ArcSDE service, the amount of shared memory to allocate to data buffers, and the amount of time to wait for a connection to the service before timing out. The giomgr.defs file is read when the ArcSDE service is started. To change a parameter, edit the file and restart the service.

A full list of the giomgr.defs parameters is provided in 'Appendix E: ArcSDE initialization parameters'. The following sections discuss in more detail some of the individual parameters and their impact on the ArcSDE service.

Session parameters

The session parameters are CONNECTIONS, TEMP, and TCPKEEPALIVE.

The CONNECTIONS parameter restricts the number of concurrent connections a single ArcSDE service will allow. However, if multiple ArcSDE services are running, setting a value for this parameter allows the ArcSDE administrator to balance the load on the system by distributing connections across all available ArcSDE services.

The CONNECTIONS parameter should not be set to higher than the total number of ArcSDE client licenses that have been purchased, as ArcSDE allocates 780 bytes of shared memory for each potential connection. The default is 64.

The TEMP parameter specifies the full path to the directory that the ArcSDE service uses for temporary things such as the shared memory file on UNIX systems and temporary storage for the attribute Binary Large Objects, or BLOBs, that are larger than specified by the BLOBMEM parameter. For more information on this parameter, please refer to the section 'Managing BLOB data' later in this chapter. A directory with at least 5 MB of available space should be specified. More space may be required for

ArcSDE services that support applications allowing users to concurrently access large binary objects stored in attribute BLOB columns.

Sometimes the computer on which an application is running crashes or a user unexpectedly terminates an application. Unless the TCPKEEPALIVE parameter is set to TRUE, the ArcSDE server does not detect the absence of the client process and does not disconnect the user. When this happens, the ArcSDE client connection remains as a license checked out, and the ArcSDE administrator must manually terminate the client process to recover it.

The TCP/IP KEEPALIVE interval is a systemwide parameter that affects not just the ArcSDE service, but every service running in the TCP/IP environment. By setting the ArcSDE TCPKEEPALIVE parameter to TRUE, the system TCP/IP KEEPALIVE settings are used. The default test interval is two hours of idle time—that is, the system checks the connected sessions every two hours. When this happens, any ArcSDE connections whose client processes have been terminated are disconnected and the licenses released. If the network environment in which the ArcSDE service operates is reliable, TCPKEEPALIVE may be set to TRUE. However, please be aware that a disconnection may be triggered by short-term network outages (~10 minutes) when TCPKEEPALIVE is set to TRUE. By default, TCPKEEPALIVE is set to FALSE.

Transport buffer parameters

After a user connects to an ArcSDE service from an application such as ArcMap™ or ArcCatalog™, they access the feature classes and tables stored in the database. Each time any of these items are accessed, an ArcSDE stream is created. An ArcSDE stream is a mechanism that transports data between the database the ArcSDE service is currently connected to and an application such as ArcMap. For example, when a user connects to an

ArcSDE service and adds three feature classes to ArcMap, three ArcSDE streams are created. For further information on streams and the parameters available to control their operation, please refer to the section 'Streams' later in this chapter.

When an ArcSDE stream is created, the ArcSDE service allocates transport buffers on both the client and the server. Transport buffers reduce I/O and improve performance by accumulating records and sending them across the network in batches rather than as individual records.

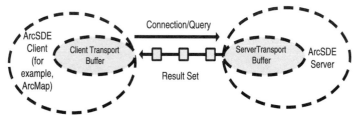

Client/Server transport buffers

The records are collected in the ArcSDE server's transport buffer and sent to the ArcSDE client transport buffer when the application is querying the database. Alternatively, the records are collected in the client's transport buffer and sent to the server's transport buffer when the application is writing data to the database.

Three parameters in the giomgr.defs file control the transport buffers.

MAXBUFSIZE   The total amount of memory allocated to each transport buffer

MINBUFSIZE   The minimum threshold of each transport buffer

MINBUFOBJECTS   The minimum number of records per transport buffer

The MAXBUFSIZE represents the total amount of memory allocated to each transport buffer. The transport buffer stops accumulating records once MAXBUFSIZE is reached and waits for the request to send the records to the other buffer.

The MINBUFSIZE and MINBUFOBJECTS parameters are lower thresholds that prevent the records from being sent until one of them is attained. For example, if the application requests data, the request is deferred until the server transport buffer reaches either MINBUFSIZE or MINBUFOBJECTS.

When creating a geodatabase, you should raise the parameters to increase the transmission speed of data loading. Once loading is complete, reduce the transport buffers.

Before raising the MAXBUFSIZE parameter too high, consider the maximum overall impact to the server's memory budget. The default MAXBUFSIZE adds 64 kilobytes per stream per ArcSDE user connection. For example, if there are 100 users using an application that displays seven feature classes, ArcSDE allocates a total of 44,800 kilobytes (100 * 7 * 64) of memory for the server's transport buffers. Doubling the MAXBUFSIZE in this example would result in 89,600 kilobytes of memory allocated to the server's transport buffers. Excessive paging may result on the server if MAXBUFSIZE is set too high and physical memory is not available to satisfy it.

Set MINBUFSIZE no more than one-half of the MAXBUFSIZE. Setting MINBUFSIZE too high increases wait time. If MAXBUFSIZE is 64K and MINBUFSIZE is 56K, the client will wait until the 56K threshold is reached before sending the transport buffer.

Reducing the MINBUFSIZE parameter improves the cooperative processing between client and server.

MINBUFOBJECTS depends on the size (bytes) of a row of data. MINBUFOBJECTS has precedence over MINBUFSIZE. If the minimum number of objects is reached before the minimum buffer size, the contents of the transport buffer are sent.

ArcSDE application developers can override the giomgr.defs transport buffer parameters with the C API function SE_connection_set_stream_spec.

1. Transfer buffer empty.

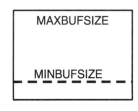

2. < MINBUFSIZE
Client sends query to server. Buffer loading begins-NO transfer to client.

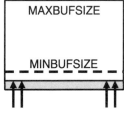

3. = MINBUFSIZE
If client is waiting, data transfer begins.

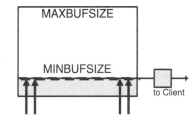

4. > MINBUFSIZE
If client is not waiting, buffer loading continues.

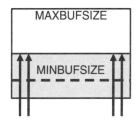

5. > MINBUFSIZE
Buffer loading continues until client is waiting again.

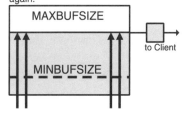

6. = MAXBUFSIZE
If client is not waiting for transfer and buffer is full, buffer loading STOPS.

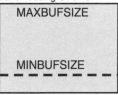

The data transfer process from an ArcSDE server transfer buffer to an ArcSDE client

Array buffer parameters

For each ArcSDE stream that is created, ArcSDE allocates an array buffer.

Whenever possible, groups of records are transferred between ArcSDE and the RDBMS server. For RDBMSs that have implemented array inserts, the ArcSDE server inserts records into the RDBMS server array. All supported RDBMSs, except Microsoft®Access, have implemented array fetch mechanisms, so whenever ArcSDE issues a select statement on behalf of the user, it fetches or gets the records in an array.

Array buffers reduce the amount of I/O occurring between ArcSDE and the RDBMS server by fetching and inserting data in larger chunks. Less I/O results in better performance. However, excessive paging can result if the array buffers are set larger than necessary. As a general rule, approximately 100 records is the optimum number of records to array process for most applications.

The array buffer parameters determine the size of the array buffers. Parameters that affect query performance are SHAPEPTSBUFSIZE, ATTRBUFSIZE, MAXARRAYSIZE, and MAXARRAYBYTES.

```
MAXARRAYSIZE      100      #Max. array fetch size

MAXARRAYBYTES   550000     #Max. array bytes
                            allocated per stream

SHAPEPTSBUFSIZE 400000     #Shape POINTS array
                            buffer size

ATTRBUFSIZE      50000     #Attribute array buffer
                            size
```

The array buffer parameters define the number of records transferred together for insert and query operations. During an array insert, ArcSDE fills the array buffer with records from the server transport buffer and transfers the entire array to the RDBMS. ArcSDE queries data in an array by using array buffers to receive the data.

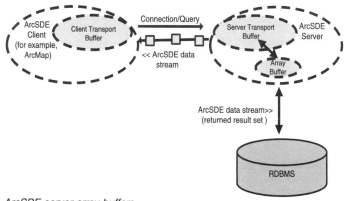

ArcSDE server array buffers

Estimating SHAPEPTSBUFSIZE

Array inserts of feature geometry are divided into two parts: feature metadata and point data. Feature metadata, including the feature ID, number of points, and entity type, requires the same amount of space for each feature. The space required to store the point data, on the other hand, varies according to the number of points in the feature.

SHAPEPTSBUFSIZE determines the buffer size for the point data. The default setting is based on an array size of 100. Tuning SHAPEPTSBUFSIZE to the optimal setting is critical to performance. The ArcSDE server estimates the average size of all features based on the array size (MAXARRAYSIZE) and the size of the points buffer (SHAPEPTSBUFSIZE). If a feature exceeds the average size, it is flagged as truncated and fetched separately.

For example, suppose SHAPEPTSBUFSIZE is 400,000 (400K), and the array size per fetch (MAXARRAYSIZE) is 100 rows (or 100 feature classes). The features in this example do not have annotation, z-values, or measures, so each point requires eight bytes (four bytes for the x-value and four bytes for the y-value).

Dividing SHAPEPTSBUFSIZE by MAXARRAYSIZE returns the maximum space available for each feature's points within the array buffer.

400000 / 100 = 4000

Further dividing the maximum space available to each feature by the number of bytes each point requires returns the total number of points that can be stored in the maximum space available to each feature.

4000 / 8 = 500

In this case, ArcSDE expects each feature to have no more than 500 points. When ArcSDE encounters features with 501 or more points, the feature is skipped and fetched separately, forcing an additional I/O fetch from the RDBMS.

Setting the SHAPEPTSBUFSIZE parameter too small results in a higher number of features to be fetched individually, which diminishes performance. Setting this parameter too high wastes memory.

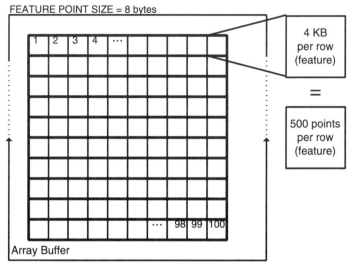

SHAPEPTSBUFSIZE = 400K

MAXARRAYSIZE = 100 ROWS (FEATURES)

FEATURE POINT SIZE = 8 bytes

The SHAPEPTSBUFSIZE and MAXARRAYSIZE parameters determine the number of points that can be stored in the maximum space available for each feature within an ArcSDE array buffer.

Point size

The number of bytes required by each point depends on its coordinate type. If the feature class only has x,y coordinates, the number of bytes each point requires is 8. If either z-values or measures are present, 12 bytes are required. If both z-values and measures are present, 16 bytes are required.

Determining 90 percent of the most queried feature classes for an optimum SHAPEPTSBUFSIZE setting

1. Determine the total number of features in the feature class by issuing this SQL query.

2. Determine the largest number of points in the feature class to use as a starting point in the step.

3. Through iteration, determine the number of points 90 percent of the features have. Start by using an x-value that is 0.75 * maximum numofpts. Increase or decrease the x-value until the feature count is 90 percent of total features.

4. Multiply the number of points by the number of rows (MAXARRAYSIZE) the array will hold and the number of bytes required by each point.

   For instance, if MAXARRAYSIZE is set to 100, 90 percent of the features have 710 or fewer points, and each point requires 8 bytes, set the SHAPEPTSBUFSIZE to 5,680,000.

1
```
select count(*) 'total features' from f<n>;
    - non-object-relational model
```
```
select count(*) 'total features' from table;
    - object relational model
```

2
```
select max(numofpts) 'maximum numofpts' from
f<n>;
```
```
select max(numpoints<spatial_column>))
'maximum numofpts' from <table>;
```

3
```
select count(*) 'feature count' from f<n>
where numofpts < X;
```
```
select count(*) 'feature count' from table
where numpoints(<spatial_column>) < X;
```

4
```
SHAPEPTSBUFSIZE = (MAXARRAYSIZE) * (number of
points) * (point size)
```
```
5680000 = 100 * 710 * 8
```

Adjusting ArcSDE service initialization parameters (continued)

Estimating ATTRBUFSIZE

ATTRBUFSIZE defines the array buffer size for attribute (non-BLOB) data. Tuning the attribute array buffer is similar to the SHAPEPTSBUFSIZE. The default 50,000 setting allows 100 rows each containing 500 bytes of attribute data.

Performance is affected when the number of rows that can be fetched into the attribute buffer does not match the MAXARRAYSIZE parameter setting. For queries involving multiple columns, add the number of bytes per column to get a total row size. If the ATTRBUFSIZE divided by row size is less than the MAXARRAYSIZE, the actual array size for the query (MAXARRAYSIZE) is less. This adjustment occurs because giomgr.defs parameters are not flexible. If the number of rows exceeds MAXARRAYSIZE, the array size remains the same.

Setting MAXARRAYSIZE

As mentioned, MAXARRAYSIZE sets the number of rows that the server will fetch per request. The recommended default value is 100. Optimal values can range between 20 and 150 on different platforms and RDBMSs. Once the shape points data (SHAPEPTSBUFSIZE) and attribute buffer (ATTRBUFSIZE) are correctly tuned, try several array sizes to determine the optimal setting for each installation.

Setting MAXARRAYBYTES

Control the maximum number of bytes per stream with the MAXARRAYBYTES parameter. This value represents the total bytes that can be allocated to both ATTRBUFSIZE and SHAPEPTSBUFSIZE for each stream.

MAXARRAYBYTES is simply a way to manage the memory allocations for array buffers on the server. The sum of ATTRBUFSIZE and SHAPEPTSBUFSIZE must be less than or equal to MAXARRAYBYTES. If it isn't, the ArcSDE service will not start. If this problem occurs, either increase MAXARRAYBYTES or decrease either ATTRBUFSIZE or SHAPEPTSBUFSIZE.

This value cannot be changed with the SE_connection_set_stream_spec function and can only be altered in the giomgr.defs file by the ArcSDE administrator.

Managing BLOB data

The BLOB parameters, MAXBLOBSIZE and BLOBMEM, determine the server-side buffer requirements for BLOB data types. MAXBLOBSIZE determines the maximum number of bytes the server will accept. A BLOB is either written to memory or disk, depending on the size. BLOBMEM determines the maximum BLOB size for in-memory storage. That is, the server allocates BLOBMEM bytes to hold the BLOB. A BLOB that exceeds this size is written to disk.

Registered tables

The REGISTRATIONS parameter controls the total number of registered tables. You must register tables accessed by an application that uses logging or if the feature class or table is versioned. The ArcSDE service allocates 504 bytes of shared memory for each entry. For instance, if REGISTRATIONS is set to 500, 252,000 bytes are allocated to the ArcSDE service.

Layers

The LAYERS parameter specifies the maximum number of feature classes the ArcSDE service supports. Set the value higher if users that create feature classes report a SE_TOO_MANY_LAYERS error. Avoid setting this parameter any higher than needed as it allocates 12 bytes of shared memory per entry.

Maximum initial features (Oracle only)

The MAXINITIALFEATS parameter controls the initial features argument that may be submitted to either the sdelayer command or the SE_layer_create function. Based on the value of initial features, sdelayer or SE_layer_create calculates the initial and next extent of the feature and spatial index table. To prevent the possibility of a user inadvertently entering a very large initial features value and thus acquiring an initial extent beyond what is needed, the administrator can limit the initial features value by setting the MAXINITIALFEATS parameter.

Statistics

The MAXDISTINCT parameter controls the number of distinct values a call to either the SE_table_calculate_stats or the SE_stream_calculate_table_statistics function can return. Setting this parameter to 0 allows an unlimited number of distinct values to be returned by the applications that call these functions. However, the distinct values are generated in memory on the server and passed to the client's memory when the list is complete. Calculating the statistics of a very large table could pose a threat to the client and server resources. A prudent database administrator will set this value high enough to allow most queries to complete but not so high as to expose the server or the client application to a memory shortage. Should a user receive the error message SE_TOO_MANY_DISTINCTS , the MAXDISTINCT parameter may be raised. Do so cautiously as this has an impact on both client and server memory. It may be

advisable to examine the applications to determine whether queries could be performed more efficiently.

Locking

The giomgr.defs file contains three parameters that control locking: LOCKS, MAXTABLELOCKS, and STATELOCKS. The default values are 10,000, which should be adequate for most applications. However, if users report an SE_OUT_OF_LOCKS error, or if that error appears in the sde.errlog file, increase the associated lock parameter.

The LOCKS parameter specifies the maximum number of area locks allowed by the ArcSDE service. If a large number of users are editing feature classes and they are receiving SE_OUT_OF_LOCKS errors, increase this parameter and restart the ArcSDE server. Each lock entry in the LOCKS parameter requires 12 bytes of shared memory, so setting this value higher has a low impact on the overall performance of the ArcSDE service.

The MAXTABLELOCKS parameter controls the maximum number of business table row locks the ArcSDE server allows. If users are updating large numbers of business table records and they receive an SE_OUT_OF_LOCKS error, increase the MAXTABLELOCKS parameter. As each table row lock entry only requires 8 bytes of memory, increasing this value has very little impact on the ArcSDE service.

The STATELOCKS parameter limits the total number of locks that may be applied to states in a versioned database. Each user that queries a versioned feature class or table is allocated a state lock. Users who edit a feature class or table receive one state lock per edit operation. After 30 states are generated, ArcSDE automatically trims the first 15 states and compresses them into the sixteenth state. However, the state locks generated within one version remain if a new version is started. State locks can accumulate for a user if they create several new versions during an edit session.

This is normal practice when versions are used as save points. If users report that they are receiving an SE_OUT_OF_LOCKS error when editing a versioned feature class or table, increase the STATELOCKS parameter. As each table lock entry requires 8 bytes of memory, setting this value higher has very little impact on overall performance.

Streams

You have read about Streams in the section 'Transport buffer parameters' earlier in this chapter. To recap briefly, each time a user accesses a feature class or business table, an ArcSDE stream is created to transfer the information between the client and the ArcSDE server. For example, when a user connects to an ArcSDE service and adds three feature classes to ArcMap, three ArcSDE streams are created. An ArcSDE stream is a mechanism that transports data between the database the ArcSDE service is connected to and an application such as ArcMap. The resources allocated to each stream are significant; it is therefore important that the ArcSDE administrator understands how they operate and how to control the impact they have on the resources of the ArcSDE host computer.

The administrator has two parameters to control the behavior of streams: MAXSTREAMS and STREAMPOOLSIZE.

MAXSTREAMS

The MAXSTREAMS parameter controls the maximum number of concurrently opened streams allowed on an ArcSDE service. If users report they have received the SE_TOO_MANY_STREAMS error, consider raising the MAXSTREAMS parameter to allow more streams to be created. However, if resources on the server, especially memory, are at a premium, first examine the applications

to determine whether some of the feature classes displayed are necessary.

Each additional stream is allocated memory by the ArcSDE service for its transport and array buffers as well as for its other structures.

STREAMPOOLSIZE

The process of creating a stream requires the allocation of memory and other resources. These are released when users close the stream, which normally happens when they disconnect from the ArcSDE service.

If the STREAMPOOLSIZE is set to a value greater than 0, ArcSDE creates a pool of released stream resources for reuse. In this case, when a user releases a stream, the ArcSDE service first checks the stream pool to determine if it is full. If it is not, the released stream resources are added to the pool; otherwise the resources are deallocated. When the same user application creates a stream, the ArcSDE service checks the stream pool for an available stream. If one exists, ArcSDE removes it from the pool and allocates it to the user application.

The STREAMPOOLSIZE parameter determines how many stream resources the stream pool should hold. If an application is designed such that users tend to connect, browse, and disconnect, set the STREAMPOOLSIZE to be at least half the size of MAXSTREAMS. On the other hand, if an application is designed such that users connect, display, and query the same data continuously, the STREAMPOOLSIZE probably does not need to be any larger than 10 percent of MAXSTREAMS.

Raster parameters

ArcSDE stores images similar to the way it stores features, in an RDBMS BLOB column. The ArcSDE system table RASTER_COLUMNS keeps track of all of the raster columns in the databases just as the LAYERS table keeps track of the feature class columns. For more information about raster tables, see 'Appendix C: ArcSDE table definitions'.

RASTERCOLUMNS

The RASTERCOLUMNS parameter determines the maximum number of raster columns the ArcSDE service allows within the database. If users report a SE_TOO_MANY_RASTERCOLUMNS error, increase the RASTERCOLUMNS parameter to allow for the creation of additional raster columns. The ArcSDE server allocates eight bytes of shared memory for each RASTERCOLUMNS entry.

RASTERBUFSIZE

The RASTERBUFSIZE parameter controls raster data transfer, which operates in a fashion similar to streamed data (see 'Transport buffer parameters' and 'Array buffer parameters' sections in this chapter).

The RASTERBUFSIZE is specified in bytes and must be large enough to hold the largest raster tile. The default ArcInfo tile size is 64 * 64 pixels. Data that are 8 bits per pixel have a tile size of 4,096 bytes (64 * 64).

The raster transfer includes both an array buffer and transport buffers. The raster array buffer is set at two times the RASTERBUFSIZE parameter, while the raster transport buffers are set to the RASTERBUFSIZE. Therefore, the memory allocated to raster transfer on the server is three times RASTERBUFSIZE. On the client, RASTERBUFSIZE bytes of memory are allocated to the client raster transport buffer. The raster buffers are allocated when raster tiles are accessed by a stream. The raster buffers are not deallocated until the stream is closed (unless the stream is added to the stream pool—see STREAMPOOLSIZE). In other words, a user can elect to display an image and a feature class together in ArcMap. The raster buffers are allocated on demand when a user selects an image stored in the feature class's business table.

If the ArcSDE service encounters a raster tile that does not fit into the transport buffer, the SE_RASTERBUFFER_TOO_SMALL error is returned. If users report this error, determine the tile size they are using. If they are using a 256 x 256 tile size on an 8-bit image, the RASTERBUFSIZE must be at least (256 * 256) 65,536 bytes. The resolution of the image must be either 16-, 32-, or 64-bit resolutions. A 64-bit resolution transferred with a tile size of 256 x 256 requires a RASTERBUFSIZE of (256 * 256 * 8) 524,288 bytes. If memory is at a premium, advise users to specify a smaller tile size rather than raise the RASTERBUFSIZE.

Maximum time difference

The maximum time difference that a client's system clock can deviate from a host's system clock can be set with the giomgr.defs MAXTIMEDIFF parameter. The parameter is specified in seconds. It prevents an unauthorized entry by individuals who may have captured a network packet with a sniffer software that contains an ArcSDE connection string. Because the encrypted password is time stamped, the packet cannot be resent at a later time if MAXTIMEDIFF is set low enough (for example, 60 seconds).

If legitimate connections receive a "-99 password received was sent 7 MAXTIMEDIFF seconds before" error, reset the client machine's system time to the host's system time. Disable MAXTIMEDIFF by setting it to -1.

Displaying the ArcSDE initialization parameters

You can list the current ArcSDE initialization parameters using the sdemon command with the "-o info -I config" options.

```
$ sdemon -o info -I config

ArcSDE I/O Manager Configuration Parameters at
Fri Apr 16 10:52:48 1999

_____

ArcSDE Version              8.0
ArcSDE Server Build         Build 374 Wed Mar
                            17 01:04:49 PST 1999
Underlying DBMS             Oracle
Max. Server Connections     64
Max. Number SDE Layer Locks100
Max. Number SDE State Locks   500
Max. Number SDE Table Locks   100
Max. Layer Number             500
Max. Registration Number      3000
Root Path                   /abbey1/sdeexe40
Temp Path                   /tmp
Min. <Transport> Buffer Size  16384 Bytes
Max. <Transport> Buffer Size  65536 Bytes
<Min. Transport Buffer Count> 512 Objects
Max. Initial Features         10000 Objects
Max. stream pool size         3 streams
Server Timeout                10 Seconds
Max. BLOB Size                1000000 Bytes
Max. in Memory BLOB Size      500000 Bytes
Max. Distincts                512
Autocommit Frequency          1000
Max. Streams                  8
Shape Point Buffer Size       400000 Bytes
Attribute Buffer Size         50000 Bytes
Blob Buffer Size              30000 Bytes
Max. Array Size               100
Max. Array Bytes              550000 Bytes
Max. Client/Server Time Diff. Unlimited
State Caching                 On
$
```

Managing ArcSDE services

4

The administrator who manages the ArcSDE service can place the service in one of three states: running, paused, or shutdown. Although it is desirable to maintain the ArcSDE service in the most productive state (that is running), at times it is necessary to shut down the service, perhaps to perform essential maintenance.

The tools you use to manage an ArcSDE service depend on whether the service has been installed on a Windows NT or UNIX system. On UNIX systems, the administrator uses the sdemon command. ArcSDE services installed on Windows NT are started and stopped from the service menu. In both cases, the sdemon command is used to pause and resume the service.

ArcSDE services installed on either Windows NT or UNIX can be managed from a remote computer using the sdemon command. However, only a remote UNIX system can manage an ArcSDE service installed on a UNIX system.

Before starting an ArcSDE service

To recap from the introduction in Chapter 2, you must satisfy several conditions before the ArcSDE service can be started.

- The RDBMS server must be up and running.
- The RDBMS ArcSDE user account must exist.
- The system environment must be set such that the ArcSDE server can connect to the RDBMS server as the ArcSDE user.
- The ArcSDE home directory must exist.
- An SdeServer license must be available for checkout from a license server accessible through the network.

Starting a local ArcSDE service on Windows NT

You can start an ArcSDE service on Windows NT from the Services menu. The name of the service always begins with "ArcSDE Service", and the ArcSDE service name itself is enclosed in parentheses—for example, ArcSDE Service(arcsde8). If the service fails to start, make a note of the Windows NT error number and see the 'Common ArcSDE startup problems on Windows NT servers' in Chapter 6, 'Troubleshooting the ArcSDE service'.

1. Open the Control Panel by clicking Start, choose Settings, and choose Control Panel.

2. Double-click Services to open the Services menu.

3. Click the ArcSDE service name and click Start.

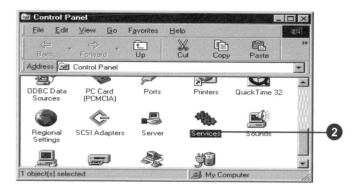

The status changes to Started, and the Start button is grayed out.

Starting a remote ArcSDE service on Windows NT

You can start a remote Windows NT ArcSDE service from another Windows NT machine.

The remote computer must be accessible over the network. The ping command can be used from an MS–DOS prompt to determine whether the remote ArcSDE service host can be reached.

Remote start up is initiated using the sdemon command from an MS–DOS command prompt. The addition of the -s <server> and -i <service> options identify the remote host computer and the name of the remote ArcSDE service.

Tip

ArcSDE administrator Windows NT user group

The ArcSDE administrator must belong to the Windows NT administrator or power user group on the remote machine and have access via the system's environment variables to the sdemon command.

See Also

For more information on the various sdemon command options, see 'Appendix D: ArcSDE command references'.

Using the ping command to verify a remote network connection

1. At the MS–DOS command prompt, type the command "ping" followed by the name or TCP/IP address of the remote computer.

```
C:\> ping bruno
Pinging bruno.esri.com [46.1.1.92] with 32
bytes of data:
Reply from 46.1.1.92: bytes=32 time<10ms
TTL=128
Reply from 46.1.1.92: bytes=32 time<10ms
TTL=128
Reply from 46.1.1.92: bytes=32 time<10ms
TTL=128
Reply from 46.1.1.92: bytes=32 time<10ms
TTL=128

C:\>
```

Starting a remote Windows NT ArcSDE service

1. To start the remote ArcSDE service, "arcsde_8", on host computer "Bruno", type the sdemon command and include the "-s bruno -i arcsde_8" options.

```
C:\>sdemon -o start -p my_password
     -s bruno -i   arcsde_8
```

Starting a local ArcSDE service on UNIX

The sdemon command manages ArcSDE services configured on UNIX systems.

Tip

Configuring the ArcSDE service on UNIX

Because the root account can run "sdemon -o start", you may configure the ArcSDE service to start automatically when booting up the UNIX system.

Tip

Starting the ArcSDE service on UNIX

You must be logged in as either the owner of the ArcSDE service's home directory, $SDEHOME, or as the user "root" to start an ArcSDE service.

Tip

The sdemon command with -p option

You may enter the password as part of the sdemon command—for example, "$ sdemon -o start -p my_password", but the password will be displayed on the screen.

1. Type the command sdemon with the "-o start" option to start the ArcSDE service.

2. You will be prompted to type in a password. This will not be displayed on the screen for system security.

1 `$ sdemon -o start`

2 `Please enter the ArcSDE DBA password:`

The sdemon command output

The first time the ArcSDE service starts, it creates the metadata tables needed for the service to operate in the <RDBMS> ArcSDE user account's default tablespace. The output of the "sdemon -o start" command will look something like this the first time the ArcSDE service is started.

```
_____
ESRI ArcSDE I/O Manager - Release 8.0 - Wed Jun
2 13:35:02 PDT 1999

_____
VERSION table created...
SPATIAL_REFERENCES table being created...
SPATIAL_REFERENCES table created...
GEOMETRY_COLUMNS table being created...
GEOMETRY_COLUMNS table created...
LAYERS table being created...
LAYERS table created...
SDEMETADATA table being created...
SDEMETADATA table created...
RASTER_COLUMNS table being created...
RASTER_COLUMNS table created...
TABLE_REGISTRY table being created...
TABLE_REGISTRY table created...
STATES table being created...
STATES table created...
VERSIONS table being created...
VERSIONS table created...
MVTABLES_MODIFIED table being created...
MVTABLES_MODIFIED table created...
RECONCILED_STATES table being created...
RECONCILED_STATES table created...
SDELOCATORS table being created...
SDELOCATORS table created...
DBMS stored procedures being created or
updated...
DBMS stored procedures created or updated...
DBMS Connection established...
RDBMS:             "Oracle"
Service Name:      "esri_sde"
SDE Service sde4_ora started Wed Jun  2 16:18:15
1999
```

For all subsequent startups, since the metadata tables have been created, the output will simply look like this:

```
_____
ESRI ArcSDE I/O Manager - Release 8.0 - Thu Jun
24 13:59:40 PST 1999

_____
Service initialized for SDE . . .
DBMS Connection established...
RDBMS:             "Oracle"
Service Name:      "esri_sde"
ArcSDE Service esri_sde started Fri Jul 16
14:44:37 1999
```

Starting a remote ArcSDE service on UNIX

Before an ArcSDE service on a UNIX system can be started from a remote UNIX or a Windows NT machine, you must complete five configuration steps.

The dbinit.sde file must contain the database connection, the license manager variables, and the library path to the ArcSDE and RDBMS dynamic libraries. By default, this file does not exist on the UNIX platform. You will need to create the file before you update it.

You must also add additional one-line entries to the /etc/services and the /etc/inetd.conf files and then reinitialize the inetd daemon.

You can then test the remote startup procedure from either a UNIX or a Windows NT computer using the sdemon command with the "-s" and "-i" options.

Tip

/etc/inetd.conf file entry
This must be a single-line entry with no carriage returns or new lines.

1. Create the $SDEHOME/etc/ dbinit.sde file. This is an example of the variables in the dbinit.sde file.

2. As the root user, duplicate the ArcSDE service name in the /etc/services file as a user datagram protocol (udp) entry that uses the same port number.

3. Again as the root user, update the /etc/inetd.conf file. Add this line to the bottom of the file.

   This is an example of an /etc/inetd.conf file.

4. As the root user, identify the relevant process using the UNIX command "ps -" piped through "grep". Reinitialize the inetd daemon by sending it a signal hang-up or SIGHUP.

   As the ArcSDE administrator, make sure the service is not started.

5. From either a UNIX or Windows NT computer, type the sdemon command with the start, server, and service name options to remotely start an ArcSDE service.

1
```
set    ORACLE_HOME=/ultra1/oracle
set    ORACLE_SID=ora8
set    LD_LIBRARY_PATH=/usr/lib:/ultra1/
       oracle/lib:/ultra1/oraexe/sdeexe80/lib
set    ESRI_LICENSE_FILE=27005@ultra
unset  TWO_TASK
```

2
```
# \etc\services

esri_sde      5151/tcp
esri_sde      5151/udp
```

3
```
<ArcSDE instance> dgram udp wait <ArcSDE home
owner> <$SDEHOME>/bin/sderemote iomgr_inetd
<$SDEHOME>

# SDE remote start-up entries.
esri_sde dgram udp wait sde /ultra1/oraexe/
sdeexe80/bin/sderemote iomgr_inetd /ultra1/
oraexe/sdeexe80
```

4
```
$ ps -u root | grep inetd
root 112  1 0  Aug 30 ? 0:08 /usr/sbin/inetd -s

$ kill -HUP 112


$ sdemon -o status
ArcSDE Instance sde4_ora Status on ultra at
Thu Sep 30 11:32:56 1999
_____

ArcSDE instance sde4_ora is not available on
ultra.
```

5
```
$ sdemon -o start -p my_password   -s
ultra -i esri_sde
ArcSDE Instance sde4_ora started Thu Jan 15
20:31:28 1970
```

Pausing, resuming, and shutting down an ArcSDE service

When the ArcSDE service is running, client applications can log in and access the database through the ArcSDE service. When the service is paused, current application connections continue, but additional application requests to connect are refused. This allows current users to complete work before the ArcSDE service is shut down. You can return a paused ArcSDE service to running mode by executing the sdemon with the resume option. When the ArcSDE server is shut down, the sdemon command notes any ArcSDE processes still running and prompts to confirm that these tasks should be terminated before continuing to shut down. Any user who knows the ArcSDE RDBMS user's password can shut down the ArcSDE service. Shutting down the ArcSDE service relinquishes all ArcSDE service processes and operating system resources. ►

Pausing the ArcSDE service (Windows NT and UNIX)

1. To pause an ArcSDE service, type the sdemon command and specify the pause option.

```
$ sdemon -o pause -p my_password
ArcSDE I/O Manager is paused, no further
connections will be allowed
```

Resuming operation (Windows NT and UNIX)

1. To resume a paused ArcSDE service, type the sdemon command and specify the resume option.

```
$ sdemon -o resume -p my_password
ArcSDE I/O Manager is Resuming, new
connections will now be allowed
```

Shutting down a local Windows NT ArcSDE service

1. Click the Start menu, click Settings, and click Control Panel. Click on Services and scroll through the list of Windows NT services to find the ArcSDE service to shut down. Click Stop to shut down the service.

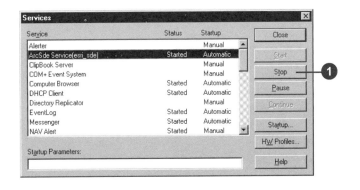

If the giomgr process stalls on a Windows NT machine and it cannot be stopped using the methods discussed, it may be necessary to terminate the process with the "killp" executable file found under %SDEHOME%\tools.

If the ArcSDE service or giomgr process stalls on a UNIX platform and it cannot be stopped, it may be necessary to terminate the process with the UNIX "kill" command.

Tip

User account permissions
Windows NT users must have power user or administrator group permissions to pause, resume, or shut down an ArcSDE service that is either local or remote.

Tip

Remotely pausing and resuming an ArcSDE service (UNIX and Windows NT)
You can use the sdemon command to remotely pause, resume, and shut down an ArcSDE service by including the remote ArcSDE server and service name with the command options—for example, "$ sdemon -o pause -p my_password -s ultra -i esri_sde".

Shutting down a stalled giomgr process on Windows NT

1. Right-click on the Windows NT taskbar and, from the menu of options that appear, click on "Task Manager...". Identify the process ID (PID) of the stalled giomgr process.

2. Type "killp" at the MS–DOS command line and include the PID obtained from the Task Manager window.

②
```
C:\> cd %SDEHOME%\tools
C:\%SDEHOME%\tools> killp 100
Do you really want to kill process with pid 100(y/n)
y
```

Shutting down a local UNIX ArcSDE service

1. Type the sdemon command with the shutdown option.

2. Type the sdemon command with the status option to confirm the ArcSDE service has been shut down.

①
```
$ sdemon -o shutdown -p my_password
ArcSDE I/O Manager is Shutdown
```

②
```
$ sdemon -o status
ArcSDE I/O Manager is not available
```

Shutting down a stalled giomgr process on UNIX

1. Identify the PID of the stalled ArcSDE service or giomgr process using the UNIX "ps - ef" command piped through "grep" to isolate the "giomgr" process.

2. Type the UNIX "kill" command and include the PID to terminate the giomgr process.

❶
```
$ ps -ef | grep giomgr
sde804 3403    1  0 06:00:03 ?      0:03 /
luke1/sdeexe80/bin/giomgr /luke1/sdeexe80
```

❷
```
$ kill -9 3403
```

Removing ArcSDE sessions (Windows NT and UNIX)

To terminate an ArcSDE user process, list all ArcSDE user processes with sdemon, locate the process identifier, and use the sdemon command with the kill option to remove the process.

Before terminating a user process, be aware that the sdemon command disconnects user processes immediately. If the termination occurs before users issue a commit on a large transaction, the changes are rolled back. This operation should be used for emergencies only such as terminating a user process that is no longer responding to the application or when a user abnormally aborts an operation while it was processing a request and the process has hung.

Removing a single ArcSDE user session

1. Locate the PID for the ArcSDE session to be terminated with the sdemon command.

2. Issue the sdemon command with the "-o kill" option and the PID.

3. Verify that the process has been terminated.

❶ `$ sdemon -o info -I users` *(list the user processes)*
```
ArcSDE Instance as8 Registered Server Tasks
on luke at Thu Sep 16 11:23:04 1999

-----------------------------------------------

PID    User  Host:OS         Started

-----------------------------------------------

90     tomb buru:Win32:XDR   Thu Sep 16 09:29:52
10627 tomb zanzi:Win32:XDR Thu Sep 16 11:12:31
```

❷ `$ sdemon -o kill -t 10627`
```
Please enter ArcSDE DBA password:

ArcSDE Instance as8 Process Management on luke
at Thu Sep 16 11:23:46 1999

-----------------------------------------------

Kill Server Task 10627?   ARE YOU SURE (Y/N)?:
y
```

❸ `$ sdemon -o info -I users` *(list the user processes)*
```
ArcSDE Instance as8 Registered Server Tasks
on luke at Thu Sep 16 11:25:04 1999

-----------------------------------------------

PID User  Host:OS          Started

-----------------------------------------------

90   tomb  buru:Win32:XDR Thu Sep 16 09:29:52
$
```

Tip

The sdemon command with the -t option

The "-t" option specifies the PID of the process to be terminated. It can also be used to terminate all current user processes by typing the "all" keyword in place of a PID.

Tip

Stalled ArcSDE user sessions

To remove stalled ArcSDE user connections or gsrvr processes that cannot be terminated with the "sdemon -o kill" command, you must use either the UNIX "kill" command or the Windows NT Task Manager.

Removing multiple ArcSDE user sessions

1. Type the sdemon -o command with the kill and -t all options.

2. Verify that all user processes have been terminated.

1 `$ sdemon -o kill -t  all`

2 `$ sdemon -o info -I users`   *(list the user processes)*

```
ArcSDE Instance as8 Registered Server Tasks
on luke at Thu Sep 16 11:25:04 1999

-------------------------------------------------

PID User  Host:OS        Started

-------------------------------------------------

There are no ArcSDE users logged in.
$
```

Monitoring ArcSDE services

5

IN THIS CHAPTER

- **Displaying ArcSDE service status and lock table information**

- **Displaying ArcSDE service statistics**

- **Displaying ArcSDE user session information**

To display the status of the ArcSDE service, use the sdemon command. This command provides a variety of administrative information including:

- The current mode of the ArcSDE service

- The number of clients using the service

- Information about each client/server connection

- Current ArcSDE service configurations

Displaying ArcSDE service status and lock table information

You can check the status of an ArcSDE service by using the sdemon command with the status option. You will see reported on-screen the current status of the service—the current connection mode and the number of active service processes.

```
$ sdemon -o status
ArcSDE Instance as8 Status on luke at Thu Sep 16
10:18:15 1999
-------------------------------------------------
Server Connection Mode:   Accepting Connections
Active Server Processes:   57
$
```

The ArcSDE locking mechanisms manage concurrent user access and guarantee read consistency when a user queries the database.

You should configure the ArcSDE service to have enough locks for the applications. Use "sdemon -o info -I locks" to keep track of the number of locks. If you find that your users' applications are approaching a lock limit set by giomgr.defs parameters, you must increase the LOCKS parameter and restart the ArcSDE service. For more information on the LOCKS parameter, refer to 'Appendix E: ArcSDE initialization parameters'.

```
$ sdemon -o info -I locks
ArcSDE Instance as8 Lock Table Information on
luke at Thu Sep 16 10:13:48 1999
-------------------------------------------------
1 PID:1017,Map Layer: 3,Lock Type: Shared Area
2 PID:1017,Map Layer: 2,Lock Type: Update Layer
-------------------------------------------------
2 of 10000 ArcSDE Layer Lock(s) currently in use.
```

```
1 PID: 1017, Object Id:  1, Object Type: 1
Application: [ArcSDE Internal]  Lock Type: Shared
Object
2 PID: 1017, Object Id:  3, Object Type: 2
Application: [User]  Lock Type: Exclusive Object
3 PID: 1017, Object Id:  2, Object Type: 1
Application: [User]  Lock Type: Shared Object
-------------------------------------------------
3 of 10000 ArcSDE Object Lock(s) currently in
use.
1   PID: 28129, State: 25685, Lock Type: Auto
Exclusive State
2   PID: 28129, State: 25684, Lock Type: Auto
Exclusive State
3   PID: 28129, State: 25683, Lock Type: Auto
Exclusive State
4   PID: 28129, State: 25682, Lock Type: Auto
Exclusive State
5   PID: 28129, State: 25681, Lock Type: Auto
Exclusive State
6   PID: 28129, State: 25680, Lock Type: Auto
Exclusive State
7   PID: 28129, State: 25679, Lock Type: Auto
Exclusive State
8   PID: 28129, State: 25685, Lock Type: Shared
State
9   PID: 28129, State: 25684, Lock Type: Shared
State
10  PID: 28129, State: 25683, Lock Type: Shared
State
11  PID: 28129, State: 25682, Lock Type: Shared
State
12  PID:    90, State: 25670, Lock Type: Auto
Exclusive State
13  PID:    90, State: 25669, Lock Type: Auto
Exclusive State
14  PID:    90, State: 25668, Lock Type: Auto
Exclusive State
15  PID:    90, State: 25667, Lock Type: Auto
Exclusive State
```

```
16 PID:    90, State: 25666, Lock Type: Auto
Exclusive State
17 PID:    90, State: 25665, Lock Type: Auto
Exclusive State
18 PID:    90, State: 25664, Lock Type: Auto
Exclusive State
19 PID:    90, State: 25670, Lock Type: Shared
State
20 PID:    90, State: 25669, Lock Type: Shared
State
21 PID:    90, State: 25668, Lock Type: Shared
State
22 PID:    90, State: 25667, Lock Type: Shared
State
23 PID:    90, State: 25666, Lock Type: Shared
State
24 PID:    90, State: 25665, Lock Type: Shared
State
25 PID:    90, State: 25664, Lock Type: Shared
State
-----------------------------------------------------

25 of  10000 ArcSDE State Lock(s) currently in
use.

1 PID: 90, table: 162, Lock Type: Shared Table
2 PID: 26732, table: 122, Lock Type: Shared
Table
3 PID: 28129, table: 162, Lock Type: Shared
Table


-----------------------------------------------------

3 of  10000 ArcSDE Table Lock(s) currently in
use.

$
```

The following lock table data appears for each lock in use:

```
PID              Identifier of the process that owns
                 the lock
```

```
MAP LAYER        Map layer number to which the
                 lock applies

LOCK TYPE        The type of lock (update/
                 shared,layer/area, auto)
```

If the lock type is an area lock or an automatic lock on a feature, the locked area also appears.

ArcSDE provides applications with four kinds of locks:

Object locks—used for versioning and geodatabase activities

Table locks—used to lock the rows of a table

Area locks—used to lock a spatial extent of a feature class

State locks—used to lock a versioned state of a feature class or table

Displaying ArcSDE service statistics

You can use the sdemon command with the stats option to display statistical information about each current ArcSDE service by using the "-o info -I stats" option:

```
$ sdemon -o info -I stats
ArcSDE Instance as8 Server Process Statistics
on luke at Thu Sep 16 10:37:14 1999
```

PID	OPS	READS	WRITES	BUFFERS	PARTIAL
90	17831	2557	958	1815	0
26732	3941	5386	3321	355	0
28129	17890	3964	969	1834	0
6796	363	59	0	37	0

F/BUF	BUF AVG	TOT Kbytes
1	14K	26732K
24	79K	28129K
2	3K	6796K
1	21K	792K

```
$
```

The output includes:

PID	Process identifier
OPS	Number of client/server operations
READS	Number of features/identifiers read from disk
WRITES	Number of features written to disk
BUFFERS	Total number of buffers sent to client task
PARTIAL	Number of features sent to client that were larger than the buffer size
F/BUF	Average number of features/identifiers per buffer
BUF AVG	Average buffer size in bytes
TOT Kbytes	Total kilobytes of data sent to client

If no processes are connected to the ArcSDE service, a message to that effect will appear.

```
$ sdemon -o info -I stats
ArcSDE Instance as8 Server Process Statistics on
luke at Thu Sep 16 10:37:14 1999

There are no ArcSDE users logged in.
$
```

Displaying ArcSDE user session information

You can list all the server process information relating to current user connections using sdemon with the "-o info -I users" options.

```
$ sdemon -o info -I users
```

ArcSDE Instance as8 Registered Server Tasks on luke at Thu Sep 16 11:10:51 1999

```
_____

PID   User   Host:OS        Started
_____

90    tomb   buru:Win32:XDR  Thu Sep 16 09:29:52
9526  tomb   zanzi:Win32:XDR Thu Sep 16 11:02:46
10406 vtest kayak:Win32:XDR Thu Sep 16 11:10:21
$
```

The following process information appears for each registered ArcSDE client.

PID   Process identifier

USER   User name of client

HOST:OS Name of the host computer and operating system

STARTED Name and time the process started

When a client terminates its ArcSDE connection, all process statistics are written to the SDEHOME/etc/giomgr.log file. The output from that file would look similar to the following:

Thu Sep 16 10:24:26 1999 - SDE Server Pid 5429 Stopped, User: sdetest.

Thu Sep 16 10:23:30 1999 - SDE Server Pid 5429 Registered, User: sdetest.

Thu Sep 16 10:24:26 1999 - Process 5429, R/T Calls 22, Features read 0, wrote 35

51, Locks 0, Buffers 5, Partial 0 , Buffered Features 3551, Buffered Data 3320K

Thu Sep 16 10:24:26 1999 - SDE Server 5429 exit'd with status 0

$

Troubleshooting the ArcSDE service

6

Most problems associated with starting an ArcSDE service occur because of a problem with the system environment. Often a critical step was missed during the installation or configuration of the software.

What happens when you start an ArcSDE service

This section describes the startup of an ArcSDE service, the problems that may occur, and their probable causes.

The ArcSDE service starts the giomgr process

The giomgr executable file must be accessible. On UNIX systems make sure that $SDEHOME\bin is in the system path and $SDEHOME\lib is in the system library path. On Windows NT, %SDEHOME%\bin must be in the system path if the sdemon command is used to start the service. Although on Windows NT the service is normally started from the services menu, sometimes it is appropriate to use the sdemon command to debug a failed startup.

The giomgr reads the system environment variables from the dbinit.sde file

The SDEHOME\dbinit.sde file contains settings for system environment variables that override those set in the system environment for either UNIX or Windows NT systems. On UNIX systems if the dbinit.sde file does not exist, the sdemon command displays a warning message during startup. For more information, see 'The dbinit.sde file format' in Chapter 3, 'Configuring ArcSDE services'.

On UNIX systems (and on Windows NT systems if the service is started from an MS–DOS command prompt using the sdemon command), the contents of the dbinit.sde file can be displayed during startup by setting the SDEDBECHO system environment variable to TRUE.

Be sure the RDBMS connection variables and the license manager variables are set correctly.

You may list the current ArcSDE environment variables by using the sdemon command with "-o info -I vars" options.

```
$ sdemon -o info -I vars

ArcSDE Instance esri_sde's environment variables on
nendrum at Mon Oct 18 10:42:48 1999
--------------------------------------------------
ARCHOME=\\install\daily\arcexe80
ARCHOME_USER=C:\Program Files\ESRI\ArcInfo
ARCINFOFONTNAME=Courier New
ARCINFOFONTSIZE=8
ATHOME=\\install\daily\arcexe80\arctools
COMPUTERNAME=NENDRUM
ComSpec=C:\WINNT\system32\cmd.exe
NUMBER_OF_PROCESSORS=1
OS=Windows_NT
Os2LibPath=C:\WINNT\system32\os2\dll;
Path=d:\oracle\bin;C:\Program
Files\Oracle\jre\1.1.7\bin;C:\WINNT\system32;C:\WINNT;C:\Program
Files\ESRI\ArcInfo\bin;D:\ESRI\ArcInfo\arcsde\bin;D:\ESRI\ArcInfo\arcsde\lib
PROCESSOR_ARCHITECTURE=x86
PROCESSOR_IDENTIFIER=x86 Family 6 Model 3
Stepping 4, GenuineIntel
PROCESSOR_LEVEL=6
PROCESSOR_REVISION=0304
SDEHOME=D:\ESRI\ArcInfo\arcsde
SystemDrive=C:
SystemRoot=C:\WINNT
USERPROFILE=C:\WINNT\Profiles\Default User
windir=C:\WINNT
SDENOEQUIV=true

$
```

The giomgr checks out an SdeServer license

Be sure the license manager is running and that an SdeServer license is available for checkout.

ArcSDE Windows NT license manager

On the Windows NT platform, the ArcSDE administrator can determine which license manager the ArcSDE service is using by examining the LICENSE_SERVER registry parameter.

Once you have identified which license manager is being used, you can check its current status by logging on to the computer that hosts the ArcSDE license manager and display the license manager status window.

The display must include an entry for the SdeServer license. The total number of licenses available for checkout and the currently checked out SdeServer licenses are also listed. Make sure there is at least one license available to check out. ▶

Examining the Windows NT LICENSE_SERVER registry parameter

1. To invoke the registry editor, click the Start menu and then click Run. Type regedt32 on the input line and click OK.

2. When the Registry Editor appears, click the HKEY_LOCAL_MACHINE window and expand SOFT-WARE, ESRI, ArcInfo, ArcSDE, and 8.0. Expand your ArcSDE product folder and open the folder bearing the name of the ArcSDE service you are trying to start. Examine the value of the LICENSE_SERVER param-eter—this will identify your license manager.

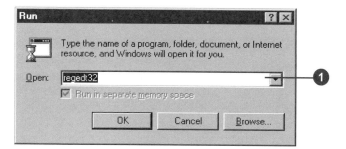

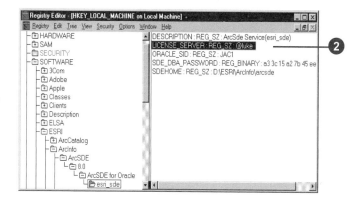

Checking the status of a Windows NT license manager

1. Log on to the computer that hosts the license manager. Click the Start menu, click Programs, click ESRI, and click on License Manager. Click on Display License Manager Status to bring up the status menu.

Listing ArcSDE license manager settings and the license manager status on UNIX

To determine which license manager the ArcSDE service is using, examine the contents of the dbinit.sde file and list the system environment settings.

On a UNIX system, you can set either the ESRI_LICENSE_FILE or LM_LICENSE_FILE variable in the dbinit.sde file to specify a license manager.

Either the ESRI_LICENSE_FILE variable or the LM_LICENSE_FILE variable may contain multiple entries separated by a colon. The giomgr process accesses the license managers as they are listed from left to right. The first license manager the giomgr process is able to access with an available SdeServer license becomes the ArcSDE service license manager. Any other entries are ignored. ▶

1. Use the "$printenv" command if you are using a C shell environment and the "$env" command if you are using a Bourne shell to list the current system environment. ▶

```
$ env
HOME=/ultra1/sde
PATH=/ultra1/sdeexe80/bin:/ultra1/app/ora815/
product/8.1.5/bin:/bin:/usr/bin:/usr/ucb:/etc:.
LOGNAME=sde
SHELL=/bin/csh
PWD=/ultra1/sde
USER=sde
ORACLE_HOME=/ultra1/app/ora815/product/8.1.5
ORACLE_SID=ora815
LM_LICENSE_FILE=27005@luke ──────────①
SDEHOME=/ultra1/sdeexe80
SDEINSTANCE=sde4_ora8i
LD_LIBRARY_PATH=/ultra1/sdeexe80/lib:/ultra1/
app/ora815/product/8.1.5/lib:/usr/dt/lib:/usr/
lib

$
```

License manager variables

If the dbinit.sde file contains an LM_LICENSE_FILE variable that seems to be ignored, check the system environment to ensure that the ESRI_LICENSE_FILE variable is not set. An ESRI_LICENSE_FILE variable set in the system environment takes precedence over an LM_LICENSE_FILE variable set in the dbinit.sde file.

2. Once you have determined which license manager the ArcSDE service uses, examine the license manager itself.

Log in to the host where the license manager is located and use "lmutil lmstat -A" to determine if the license server is running and if an SdeServer license is available. The available and currently checked out SdeServer licenses are listed.

```
$ lmutil lmstat -A

lmutil-Copyright (C) 1989-1998 Globetrotter
Software, Inc.

Flexible License Manager status on Tue 10/19/1999
11:20

License server status: 27005@luke
    License file(s) on luke: /luke1/sde40shadow/
oraexe/sdeexe40/sysgen/license.dat:

    luke: license server UP (MASTER) v6.1

Vendor daemon status (on luke):

    ESRI: UP v6.1

Feature usage info:

Users of SdeServer: (Total of 2 licenses
available)

    "SdeServer" v3.000, vendor: ESRI

    floating license

sde8 luke /dev/tty (v3.000) (luke/27005 5536),
start Tue 10/19 6:47


Users of SdeClient: (Total of 100 licenses
available)


    "SdeClient" v3.000, vendor: ESRI

    floating license

sde hubble sde8 (v3.000) (luke/27005 386), start
Sun 10/17 6:52 dnc styx sde8 (v3.000) (luke/27005
485), start Tue 10/19 8:14 vtest styx sde8
(v3.000) (luke/27005 1494), start Tue 10/198:14
gdb obiwan sde8 (v3.000) (luke/27005 5333), start
Tue 10/19    8:47
vtest jedi sde8 (v3.000) (luke/27005 1721), start
Tue 10/19 9:27
avtest sphinx sde8 (v3.000) (luke/27005 122),
start Tue 10/19 9:42

$
```

What happens when you start an ArcSDE service (continued)

The giomgr reads the TCP/IP service name

On Windows NT platforms, the service name is read from the registry if the ArcSDE service started from the Services menu. However, when debugging a startup problem by using the "sdemon -o start" command, the service name is read from the services.sde file.

On UNIX platforms, the service name is always read from the $SDEHOME\etc\services.sde file.

The giomgr attaches to TCP/IP port assigned to service name

The service name must be in the system's services file. On Windows NT, the ArcSDE installation program adds the service name to the system service file automatically. On UNIX platforms the services file must be updated manually.

The giomgr connects to the RDBMS using connection information from dbinit.sde and operating system environment variables

Make sure the RDBMS is up and running and that the sde user can connect to the database. The RDBMS connection parameters set in the dbinit.sde file have precedence over any parameters that are set in the system environment.

For the initial startup, the giomgr creates the data dictionary tables

The first time ArcSDE service starts up on a database, it creates the data dictionary. The ArcSDE RDBMS user creates and owns the tables and indexes that make up the data dictionary. Make sure the ArcSDE user has the necessary RDBMS permissions to create and insert records into a table and create an index on that table. About 40 MB of tablespace is required for the data dictionary.

The giomgr listens for connections on its TCP/IP port

At this point the ArcSDE service has started. Applications can now connect and use the service.

What happens when an ArcSDE application connects

This section describes the sequence of events that take place when an ArcSDE client application connects to an ArcSDE service.

The giomgr process listens for connections on its TCP/IP port

The giomgr must be in a listening state before it can process a connection request. Make sure the ArcSDE service is started and listening. Use "sdemon -o status" to determine the state of the giomgr process.

Applications submit connection requests to the ArcSDE service

The giomgr process responds to connection requests serially. Depending on the underlying RDBMS, the giomgr process may require anywhere from 1 to 5 seconds to validate a connection request. It's possible that if many applications are trying to obtain an ArcSDE connection at the same time, some may exceed the standard TCP/IP 75 second time-out. This may be prevented from happening by setting the SDEATTEMPTS environment. SDEATTEMPTS specifies the number of times an application should retry the connection.

The giomgr compares the application computer's clock time with its host's clock time

If the application computer's clock time is more than MAXTIMEDIFF seconds from the ArcSDE server's clock time, the giomgr process does allow the application to connect. MAXTIMEDIFF is set in the giomgr.defs file. See Chapter 3, 'Configuring ArcSDE services', and 'Appendix E: ArcSDE initialization parameters' for more information.

The giomgr compares the application's client ArcSDE release with the ArcSDE service's release

If the application's release is greater than the ArcSDE service's release, the connection is refused.

ArcSDE applications are downward compatible. Applications developed with the ArcSDE 8 API can connect to both ArcSDE 8 and SDE® 3 services. Applications built with the SDE 3 API cannot connect to ArcSDE 8 services. Check the application's documentation for supported ArcSDE releases.

The giomgr process starts a gsrvr process that will serve the application

The giomgr process must be able to spawn a gsrvr process. If the maximum number of processes determined by current operating system restrictions has been reached, this operation will fail and no gsrvr process will be created.

The giomgr process checks out an SdeClient license

An SdeClient license must be available for checkout. Consult the ArcInfo *License Manager's Guide* for instructions on determining the availability of such a license.

The gsrvr process attaches to shared memory

Sufficient memory must be available on the ArcSDE service's host computer. Otherwise, the application connection will fail with a shared memory error. Should this happen, make more memory available to the gsrvr processes by reconfiguring either the ArcSDE service or the RDBMS server to use less memory. If possible, add more physical memory to the host computer.

The gsrvr process connects to the RDBMS

The application must provide a valid user name, password, and database name (optional for some RDBMSs) when it submits the connection request to the giomgr process. Invalid entries are rejected with a "-9 SE_INVALID_USER" error.

The gsrvr process opens the RDBMS log file

ArcSDE applications often keep a log of table and feature class records that represent selected sets. Refer to the sdelog command in 'Appendix D: ArcSDE command references' for more information. These logs are maintained in two tables, SDE_LOGFILES and SDE_LOGFILE_DATA , and are created in the user's default tablespace when they connect to the ArcSDE service for the first time. If the gsrvr process cannot create these tables, the connection will fail.

The giomgr process attaches the application to the gsrvr process

Once the giomgr process has attached the application to the gsrvr process, its resumes listening for new connections and performing other ArcSDE service management tasks. All application communication with the RDBMS is conducted through the gsrvr process.

Common ArcSDE startup problems on UNIX servers

The following section lists some of the ArcSDE service startup problems that are likely to be encountered in a UNIX environment.

System path variable issues

- If the PATH environment variable does not include the $SDEHOME/bin directory, the following error message is reported:

  sdemon: Command not found

- If the library path environment variable does not include the $SDEHOME/lib directory, the following error message is reported:

  ld.so.1: sdemon: fatal: libsde80.so: open failed: No such file or directory

  Killed

- If the library path environment does not include the necessary RDBMS library directory, an error message similar to the following is reported:

  ld.so.1: /ultra1/ora8iexe/bin/giomgr: fatal: libclntsh.so.8.0: open failed: No such file or directory

  Killed

  Could not start ArcSDE — Check Network, $SDEHOME disk, DBMS settings and dbinit.sde.

  For more information on how to set the library environment variable for your ArcSDE product, see the *install_guide.pdf* file in the SDEHOME/documentation directory.

ArcSDE service already started

- If the I/O manager is already running, the following message appears:

  SDE Already Running

ArcSDE License Manager is not available/running

- If the license manager is not started, the following error message is reported:

  SDE servers do not appear to be licensed.
  Licensing failure, unable to continue.
  License Service Program has died! Exiting...
  Could not start ArcSDE — Check Network, $SDEHOME disk, DBMS settings and dbinit.sde.

- If an SdeServer license is not available, the following error message is returned:

  All SDE Server Licenses are in use.
  License Service Program has died! Exiting...
  Could not start ArcSDE — Check Network, $SDEHOME disk, DBMS settings and dbinit.sde.

Temporary file permission problems

- If any ArcSDE temporary files exist and they are not owned by the ArcSDE administrator, the following error message is returned:

  ERROR: Cannot Initialize Shared Memory (-79)
  Delete /tmp/<service name> and /tmp<service name>.lock if present.
  Could not start ArcSDE — Check Network, $SDEHOME disk, DBMS settings and dbinit.sde.

  Delete the temporary files /tmp/<service name> and /tmp/<service name>.lock. For example, if the service name is esri_sde, you would delete the files /tmp/esri_sde and

/tmp/esri_sde.lock. You may have to log in as the root user to delete these files.

Problems relating to the RDBMS

- If the RDBMS is not started, you will receive an error message similar to the following:

```
init_DB DB_instance_open_as_dba: -51
DBMS error code: 1034
ORA-01034: ORACLE not available
```

```
Could not start ArcSDE - Check Network,
$SDEHOME disk, DBMS settings and dbinit.sde.
```

- If the sde RDBMS password is not correct, you will receive an error message similar to the following:

```
init_DB DB_instance_open_as_dba: -93
DBMS error code: 1017
ORA-01017: invalid username/password; login
denied
```

```
Could not start ArcSDE - Check Network,
$SDEHOME disk, DBMS settings and dbinit.sde.
```

- If the sde RDBMS user does not exist, you will receive an error message similar to the following:

```
init_DB DB_instance_open_as_dba: -93
DBMS error code: 1017
ORA-01017: invalid username/password; login
denied
```

```
Could not start ArcSDE - Check Network,
$SDEHOME disk, DBMS settings and dbinit.sde.
```

Common ArcSDE startup problems on Windows NT servers

Normally the ArcSDE service is started as a Windows NT service from the services control panel. If an error appears after clicking the Start button for the ArcSDE service, try to determine the nature of the problem. The error message contains an error number.

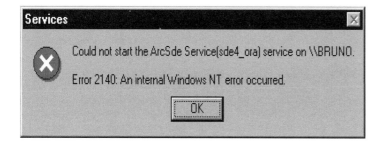

The error number generally relates to a specific type of error. Listed below are the error numbers you often encounter when starting an ArcSDE service and their likely cause.

1068 Dependency failure

The RDBMS that the ArcSDE service is trying to connect to could not be found. The most likely causes of this problem are:

- The RDBMS service is not started.

- The RDBMS server has been removed.

- The RDBMS connection information, entered when the ArcSDE server was created, is incorrect.

Make sure the RDBMS service is started and independently confirm that this is not the source of the problem. If the error persists, use the sdeservice comand to delete the existing ArcSDE service and re-create it. See the discussion of the sdeservice command in 'Appendix D: ArcSDE command references'.

1069 Login failure

Generally, this error implies the Windows NT user who started the ArcSDE service is neither a Windows NT administrator nor a power user. An incorrect password is another possibility.

If the system administrator account is not being used to start the service, make sure the user account is a member of the administrator or power user group.

Verifying Windows NT user permissions

1. Click the Start menu, click Settings, click Control Panel, and double-click the Services icon. On the Services menu, double-click the ArcSDE service entry to bring up the service menu.

2. Verify that the password is correct by reentering it.

Checking Windows NT user group permissions

1. Click the Start menu, click Programs, click AdministrativeTools, and click User Manager. Double-click on the user's name to bring up the User Properties menu.

2. Click the Groups button on the User Properties menu. Check to see if the user is in either the Administrators or Power Users group as shown in the "Member of" list.

1072 Registry was busy

Something is happening in the registry regarding the ArcSDE Service entry. Perhaps "sdeservice -o delete" was run or the service has been opened with the registry editor, regedt32. The ODBC driver version may also be incorrect. Consult the installation guide for the correct version of the ODBC driver.

1075 Service dependency deleted

The ArcSDE service is unable to locate the RDBMS service that it will connect to.

Make sure the RDBMS service exists and is started. If the problem persists, use the sdeservice command to delete and re-create the ArcSDE service. See 'Appendix D: ArcSDE command references'.

2140 Internal Windows NT error

The ArcSDE service wasn't able to complete the startup process. Examine the %SDEHOME%\etc\sde.errlog file for possible clues as to why the ArcSDE service will not start.

Possible causes include:

- Can't connect to the RDBMS server
- Can't create the ArcSDE data dictionary
- Can't check out an SdeServer license from the license server

Possible solutions include:

- If the ArcSDE user's password was entered incorrectly, use sdeservice -o modify -r SDE_DBA_PASSWORD to correct it.
- If the RDBMS connection information is incorrect, edit the %SDEHOME%\etc\dbinit.sde file.

- If an SdeServer license cannot be checked out from the license server, make sure the license manager is running and that an SdeServer license is available.

2186

This error is usually caused by a problem with the license manager.

Check the hardware key. It may not be seated correctly or is not plugged into the host computer's parallel port. This error is also returned for general license manager problems. After checking the hardware key, refer to the tools provided with the license manager and to the license manager documentation located in the SDEHOME\documentation directory.

The Windows NT Event Viewer

The Windows NT Event Viewer provides diagnostic information that may also help explain ArcSDE startup problems.

Although the Event Viewer will often include a description of the problem, you can also check the %SDEHOME%\etc\sde.errlog file. This file will contain further information relating to the Windows NT startup problems.

Using the Event Viewer

1. Click the Start menu, click Programs, click Administrative Tools, and click the Event Viewer option. From the Event Viewer menu, click Application from the Log pulldown menu to list application events. Look for a red "stop" sign icon in the Date column and the corresponding name of the ArcSDE service in the Source column. Double-click the ArcSDE service entry to bring up the Event Detail menu.

2. The Event Detail menu includes a description of the problem. In this example, it is clear that a connection to the RDBMS failed.

Examining the ArcSDE error log files

ArcSDE and all supported RDBMSs track their activities by writing messages of events to log files. The log files may be examined to trace errors that have occurred. ArcSDE writes to two log files, the giomgr.log file and the sde.errlog file.

Viewing the giomgr.log file

The giomgr.log file is a text file that contains an entry for all giomgr process activity. Each time a user connects or attempts to connect to the ArcSDE service, a message is logged. When the user disconnects, another message is logged. The giomgr.log file also captures the startup and shutdown procedures of the ArcSDE service.

Viewing the sde.errlog file

Whenever a gsrvr process encounters a problem, the ArcSDE service records an entry in the sde.errlog. Sometimes the messages are warnings, while other times they point to ArcSDE service errors that should be addressed. When examining the sde.errlog file, keep in mind that the messages written to this file only occur on the server. Sometimes an ArcSDE application will report an ArcSDE-related problem, but this event will not appear in the sde.errlog.

The sde.errlog is truncated each time the ArcSDE service is started.

RDBMS error log files

Each RDBMS has its own way of logging errors. Consult the relevant RDBMS administration guide to determine how your RDBMS logs errors.

ArcSDE I/O intercept

If you need to contact ESRI technical support, the analyst may ask you to intercept the client or server I/O, depending on the nature of the problem. ArcSDE I/O intercept captures information that the client or server sends across the TCP/IP port to a file for examination.

If this information is required, set the relevant variables in the dbinit.sde file (see details below) and restart the ArcSDE service. The dbinit.sde file is located in the $SDEHOME/etc directory on UNIX systems and in the %SDEHOME%\etc directory on Windows NT systems.

To stop intercepting ArcSDE server I/O, either comment out the variables by preceding the entry with the pound sign character "#" or delete them from the dbinit.sde file and restart the ArcSDE service.

To intercept ArcSDE client I/O, set the variables in the client application user's system environment before connecting to the ArcSDE service. To stop intercepting ArcSDE client I/O, disconnect the application from the ArcSDE service, unset the variables, and then reconnect to the ArcSDE service.

You may set the SDEINTERCEPT variable with the following flags to intercept I/O :

c —intercept the API command name

r—intercept the Channel I/O read only

w —intercept the Channel I/O write only

t—intercept log time (minute:second)

T—intercept log time (hour:minute:second)

f—intercept flush immediate

For both client and server intercepts, set the SDEINTERCEPTLOC variable to the full pathname of the filename prefix that receives the information. Information is intercepted on a per-session basis. When I/O intercept is enabled, a new file is created and written to each time an application connects to the ArcSDE service. The file is closed only after the application disconnects. ArcSDE generates a filename from the prefix provided in SDEINTERCEPTLOC by appending a numeric extension that begins at .001 and that increments sequentially for each new file created.

If the technical support analyst has asked for this intercept I/O from both the client and server, use distinct prefix names to distinguish between the client and server. For example, setting SDEINTERCEPTLOC to d:\tmp\sde_server in the dbinit.sde file captures server I/O. Setting SDEINTERCEPTLOC to d:\tmp\sde_client in the applications environment captures client I/O in the same directory but with a different prefix.

This is an example of the environment variables required to intercept server I/O from an ArcSDE service installed on Windows NT. These variables would be set in the %SDEHOME%\etc\dbinit.sde file but would not take effect until the ArcSDE service is restarted.

```
set SDEINTERCEPT=crwtf
set SDEINTERCEPTLOC=D:\tmp\sde_server
```

Following the ArcSDE service restart, any subsequent application connects to the ArcSDE service will each create a file in the D:\tmp directory with the prefix sde_server. These files will contain the server I/O generated during the application's ArcSDE session.

Appendix A: ArcSDE home directory

This appendix contains information about the ArcSDE home directory (SDEHOME) and the files installed in each subdirectory. It also includes details on switching the ArcSDE client executable image on a UNIX platform.

ArcSDE home directory (SDEHOME)

The ArcSDE home directory or SDEHOME, sdeexe80, contains the following subdirectories and files.

Directory	Contents
bin	Contains all ArcSDE 8 executable programs
etc	Contains all extra system files
include	Contains all ArcSDE client include files
lib	Contains libraries
locale	Contains National Language Support files
ssa	Directory for server-side applications
sysgen	Contains license manager files (UNIX only)
	(The default license manager files on Windows NT platforms are located in C:\Program Files\ESRI\License.)
tools	Contains DBMS tools

bin	Description
cov2sde	Converts coverage to layers
giomgr	I/O manager process executable
gsrvr	On UNIX systems it is a link to either gsrvr.shared or gsrvr.static. On Windows NT systems it is the ArcSDE server executable.
gsrvr.shared	Shared version of the ArcSDE server executable
gsrvr.static	Static version of the ArcSDE server executable
sde2cov	ArcSDE-to-coverage converter
sde2shp	ArcSDE-to-shape converter
sde2tbl	Converts ArcSDE tables to other DBMS table formats
sdeexport	Creates export files of ArcSDE layers
sdegroup	Combines shapes into multipart shapes
sdeimport	Imports ArcSDE export files
sdelayer	Manages layers
sdelicserv	Used with the license manager
sdelog	Manages logfiles
sdemon	Manages the ArcSDE server and processes
sderelease	Lists release and upgrades server version
sdetable	Manages business tables
sdeversion	Manages versioned tables

bin	Description (continued)
sdexinfo	Lists ArcSDE export file information
shp2sde	Shape-to-ArcSDE converter
shpinfo	Displays shapefile statistics
tbl2sde	Converts RDBMS table formats to ArcSDE tables
AfLockMgr.dll	Provides file locking for all applications running on the same host PC
dforrt.dll	Shared FORTRAN library (Windows NT only)
edge32.dll	Shared ArcInfo library (Windows NT only)
libloceng.dll	Shared ArcInfo library (Windows NT only)
libmtchloc.dll	Shared ArcInfo library (Windows NT only)
libxyloc.dll	Shared ArcInfo library (Windows NT only)
mtch.dll	Shared ArcInfo library (Windows NT only)
sdbase.dll	Shared ArcInfo library (Windows NT only)
sdfeat.dll	Shared ArcInfo library (Windows NT only)
sdgridio.dll	Shared ArcInfo library (Windows NT only)
sdshape.dll	Shared ArcInfo library (Windows NT only)
sdelocator	Manages locators
jsde80.dll	Shared Java™ library (Windows NT only)
pe80.dll	Shared projection run-time library (Windows NT only)
ras80.dll	Shared raster run-time library (Windows NT only)

bin	Description (continued)
sde80.dll	Shared run-time library (Windows NT only)
sdesrvr80.dll	Shared run-time library (Windows NT only)
sde80_trace.dll	Shared function trace library (Windows NT only)
sg80.dll	Shared shape geometry run-time library (Windows NT only)

etc	Description
dbinit.sde	Contains the DBMS connection information
dbtune.sde	The configuration keyword parameter file
giomgr.defs	Text file containing the ArcSDE service configuration parameters
giomgr.log	Messages from giomgr process
services.sde	ArcSDE TCP/IP service name
sde.errlog	Contains error messages from giomgr and gsrvr processes
sde.outlog	Contains output messages from gsrvr processes
sdelic.log	Contains any error messages from the license manager

include	Description
pe.h	Projection Engine data structures/types and functions
pe_coordsys_from_prj.h	
	Projection Engine predefined objects
pedef.h	Projection Engine predefined objects
pef.h	Projection Engine functions for predefined objects
sdeerno.h	Error codes include file
sderaster.h	Raster include file
sdetype.h	ArcSDE data structures/types
sg.h	Shape data structures/types
sgerr.h	Shape error include file

lib	Description
jsde80.jar	Java client archive file (UNIX)
jsde80.lib	Export Java library (Windows NT only)
libpe80.a	Static library for projection engine library
libpe80.sl	Shared library for projection engine (HP® only)
libpe80.so	Shared library for projection engine (all UNIX except HP)
libras80.a	Static library for rasters library (UNIX)
libras80.sl	Shared library for rasters (HP only)
libras80.so	Shared library for rasters (all UNIX except HP)
libsde80.a	Static library (UNIX)
libsde80.sl	Shared run-time library (HP only)
libsde80.so	Shared run-time library (all UNIX except HP)
libsde80_trace.a	Static library for function tracing library (UNIX)
libsde80_trace.sl	Shared run-time library for function tracing (HP only)
libsde80_trace.so	Shared run-time library for function tracing (all UNIX except HP)
libsdesrvr80.sl	Shared run-time library (HP only)
libsdesrvr80.so	Shared run-time library (all UNIX except HP)
libsg80.a	Static shape geometry library (UNIX)
libsg80.sl	Shared shape geometry library (HP only)
libsg80.so	Shared shape geometry library (all UNIX)
make.include	UNIX platform-dependent file for compiler/link options

lib	Description (continued)
metadata_util.spb	Stored procedure for user metadata maintenance
metadata_util.sps	Stored procedure for user metadata maintenance
pe80.lib	Export library for pe40.dll (Windows NT only)
ras80.lib	Export library for ras40.dll (Windows NT only)
sde80.lib	Export library for sde40.dll (Windows NT only)
sde80_trace.lib	Export library for sde40_trace.dll (Windows NT only)
sg80.lib	Export library for sg40.dll (Windows NT only)
xdr80.lib	Export library for the xdr40.dll
layers_util.spb	Stored procedure for layer maintenance
layers_util.sps	Stored procedure for layer maintenance
locator_util.spb	Stored procedure for locator maintenance
locator_util.sps	Stored procedure for locator maintenance
registry_util.spb	Stored procedure for registry maintenance
registry_util.sps	Stored procedure for registry maintenance
sde_util.sps	Stored procedure for ArcSDE maintenance
sref_util.spb	Stored procedure for spatial reference maintenance
sref_util.sps	Stored procedure for spatial reference
version_util.spb	Stored procedure for version maintenance
version_util.sps	Stored procedure for version maintenance

locale (UNIX) Description

codepage	Various codepage files
msg	Error message files

ssa Description

liblocssa.dll	Plug-in file for geocoding operations

sysgen (UNIX) Description

ESRI	License daemon
adminlicense	Utility to help verify the license.dat file (UNIX only)
license.boot	Scripts to automatically start the license manager during a reboot (UNIX only)
license.boot_HP11	
	Scripts to automatically start the license manager during a reboot (HP only)
license.dat	License file used by the ESRI daemon to control licenses (UNIX only)
mgrd	Starts the ESRI daemon
lmtools	FLEXlm utility program to manage the license manager
lmutil	FLEXlm utility program to manage the license file

sysgen (UNIX) Description (continued)

sample.dat	Sample license.dat file
SDE.lic	License file used by the ESRI daemon to control licenses (Windows NT only)

tools Description

generic	Directory that contains layer maintenance tools
generic/load_to_normal	
	Sample script that converts a layer from load_only_io mode to normal_io mode
<rdbms>	Directory that contains RDBMS-specific maintenance and monitoring tools
gdbs	Executable file that creates metadata tables required by ArcInfo 8
killp	Executable file to terminate stalled ArcSDE processes (Windows NT only)

ArcSDE client executable image (UNIX only)

The ArcSDE service creates a gsrvr process for each client application connected to the service. These processes respond to requests from the client applications. Each process runs until the application program terminates or the program makes a call to terminate the ArcSDE session.

The UNIX ArcSDE software has two types of gsrvr executables: a static image, gsrvr.static, and a shared image, gsrvr.shared, both of which are found in the $SDEHOME/bin directory.

All code sections of the static image are statically linked. The resulting image is relatively large and requires more memory to execute, but it is fast.

The shared image uses shared libraries from the operating system, the underlying RDBMS, and the ArcSDE service. As a result, the shared image is substantially smaller and uses fewer resources.

If you wish to switch to a shared client executable image, execute the following commands (remember to log in to the system as the ArcSDE administrator):

```
$ cd $SDEHOME/bin
$ rm gsrvr
$ ln -s gsrvr.shared gsrvr
```

To change to a static executable image, execute the following commands:

```
$ cd $SDEHOME/bin
$ rm gsrvr
$ ln -s gsrvr.static gsrvr
```

By default, the installation on UNIX sets up the ArcSDE service to use the shared image. Do not attempt to switch executable images until the ArcSDE service has been shut down.

Appendix B: ArcSDE data dictionary

The ArcSDE data dictionary includes tables that maintain information about the feature classes and feature datasets. The feature class and feature dataset spatial references, states, and versions are also maintained within the ArcSDE data dictionary. The ArcSDE data dictionary combines both the ArcSDE system tables, created by the giomgr process when the ArcSDE service is started for the first time, and the geodatabase system tables, created by the gdbs executable file (located in the SDEHOME\tools directory).

ArcSDE creates and maintains these tables and views. They were not designed to be accessed by external programs. Changing the data within the ArcSDE data dictionary, either by an external program or manually, is not supported.

The purpose of illustrating the structure of the data dictionary here is to provide an inventory of database objects that must be backed up for later restoration in the event of system failure.

ArcSDE system tables

For each ArcSDE service, the ArcSDE software creates several system tables within the ArcSDE user's schema to manage spatial data.

The ArcSDE for SQLSERVER product prefixes each of these tables with SDE_.

VERSION table

The VERSION table maintains information about the ArcSDE version with which the database expects to operate. The table contains the specific release identification for the most recent version of ArcSDE that executed a version update. The ArcSDE giomgr process checks this table to ensure proper version compatibility.

The VERSION table and other ArcSDE system tables are updated by the sdeversion program after a new version of ArcSDE is installed.

VERSION

Name	Data_Type	Null?
major	SE_INTEGER	NOT NULL
minor	SE_INTEGER	NOT NULL
bugfix	SE_INTEGER	NOT NULL
description	SE_STRING_TYPE(96)	NOT NULL
release	SE_INTEGER	NOT NULL

LAYERS table

The LAYERS table maintains data about each feature class in the database. The information helps to build and maintain spatial indexes, ensure proper shape types, and store the spatial reference for the coordinate data.

It includes the following information:

- Owner, table, and column name for the shape column
- Name of the table containing the actual shape data
- Spatial index grid cell sizes
- Envelope (minx, miny, maxx, maxy)
- ArcSDE assigned layer ID for internal use
- Feature class description
- Statistical information on the shapes in the feature class for data transfer buffer configurations

LAYERS

Name	Data_Type	Null?
Layer_id	SE_INTEGER_TYPE	NOT NULL
Description	SE_STRING_TYPE(65)	NULL
Database_name	SE_STRING_TYPE(32)	NULL
Owner	SE_STRING_TYPE(32)	NOT NULL
Table_name	SE_STRING_TYPE(160)	NOT NULL
Spatial_column	SE_STRING_TYPE(32)	NOT NULL
eflags	SE_INTEGER_TYPE	NOT NULL
Layer_mask	SE_INTEGER_TYPE	NOT NULL
gsize1	SE_FLOAT_TYPE	NOT NULL
gsize2	SE_FLOAT_TYPE	NOT NULL
gsize3	SE_FLOAT_TYPE	NOT NULL

LAYERS (continued)

Name	Data_Type	Null?
minx	SE_FLOAT_TYPE	NULL
miny	SE_FLOAT_TYPE	NULL
maxx	SE_FLOAT_TYPE	NULL
maxy	SE_FLOAT_TYPE	NULL
cdate	SE_INTEGER_TYPE	NOTNULL
layer_config	SE_STRING_TYPE(32)	NULL
optimal_array_size	SE_INTEGER_TYPE	NULL
stats_date	SE_INTEGER_TYPE	NULL
minimum_id	SE_INTEGER_TYPE	NULL
srid	SE_INTEGER_TYPE	NOTNULL
base_layer_ID	SE_INTEGER_TYPE	NOTNULL

GEOMETRY_COLUMNS table

The GEOMETRY_COLUMNS table contains the feature class names, its geometry's storage type, and coordinate dimension.

GEOMETRY_COLUMNS

Name	Data_Type	Null?
F_table_catalog	SE_STRING_TYPE(32)	NULL
F_table_schema	SE_STRING_TYPE(32)	NOTNULL
F_table_name	SE_STRING_TYPE(160)	NOTNULL
F_geometry_column	SE_STRING_TYPE(32)	NOTNULL
G_table_catalog	SE_STRING_TYPE(32)	NULL
G_table_schema	SE_STRING_TYPE(32)	NOTNULL
G_table_name	SE_STRING_TYPE(160)	NOTNULL
storage_type	SE_INTEGER_TYPE	NULL
geometry_type	SE_INTEGER_TYPE	NULL
coordinate_dimension	SE_INTEGER_TYPE	NULL
max_ppr	SE_INTEGER_TYPE	NULL
srid	SE_INTEGER_TYPE	NOTNULL

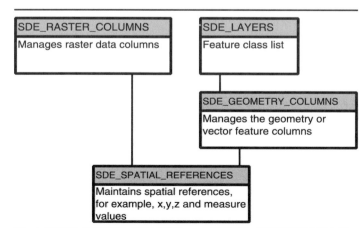

The LAYERS, RASTER_COLUMNS, and SPATIAL_REFERENCES tables

RASTER_COLUMNS table

The RASTER_COLUMNS table contains a list of raster columns stored in the database. The table and raster column names, the owner, creation date, description, database name, configuration keyword, and minimum ID. The database name is required for some RDBMS systems.

RASTER_COLUMNS

Name	Data_Type	Null?
Rastercolumn_id	SE_INTEGER_TYPE	NOT NULL
description	SE_STRING_TYPE(65)	NULL
database_name	SE_STRING_TYPE(32)	NULL
owner	SE_STRING_TYPE(32)	NOT NULL
table_name	SE_STRING_TYPE(160)	NOT NULL
raster_column	SE_STRING_TYPE(32)	NOT NULL
cdate	SE_INTEGER_TYPE	NOT NULL
config_keyword	SE_STRING_TYPE(32)	NULL
minimum_id	SE_INTEGER_TYPE	NULL
base_rastercolumn_id	SE_INTEGER_TYPE	NOT NULL
rastercolumn_mask	SE_INTEGER_TYPE	NOT NULL
srid	SE_INTEGER_TYPE	NULL

SPATIAL_REFERENCES table

The SPATIAL_REFERENCES table contains the coordinate system and floating point-to-integer transformation values. Internal functions use the parameters of a spatial reference system to translate and scale each floating point coordinate of the geometry into 32-bit positive integers prior to storage. Upon retrieval, the coordinates are restored to their original external floating point format.

SPATIAL_REFERENCES

Name	Data_Type	Null?
srid	SE_INTEGER_TYPE	NOT NULL
description	SE_STRING_TYPE(64)	NULL
auth_name	SE_STRING_TYPE(256)	NULL
auth_srid	SE_INTEGER_TYPE	NULL
falsex	SE_FLOAT_TYPE	NOT NULL
falsey	SE_FLOAT_TYPE	NOT NULL
xyunits	SE_FLOAT_TYPE	NOT NULL
falsez	SE_FLOAT_TYPE	NOT NULL
zunits	SE_FLOAT_TYPE	NOT NULL
falsem	SE_FLOAT_TYPE	NOT NULL
munits	SE_FLOAT_TYPE	NOT NULL
srtext	SE_STRING_TYPE(1024)	NOT NULL

TABLE_REGISTRY table

The TABLE_REGISTRY table manages all registered tables. The values include an ID, table name, owner, and description.

TABLE_REGISTRY

Name	Data_Type	Null?
registration_id	SE_INTEGER_TYPE	NOT NULL
table_name	SE_STRING_TYPE(160)	NOT NULL
Owner	SE_STRING_TYPE(32)	NOT NULL
rowid_column	SE_STRING_TYPE(32)	NULL
description	SE_STRING_TYPE(65)	NULL
object_flags	SE_INTEGER_TYPE	NOT NULL
registration_date	SE_INTEGER_TYPE	NOT NULL
config_keyword	SE_STRING_TYPE(32)	NULL
minimum_id	SE_INTEGER_TYPE	NULL
imv_view_name	SE_STRING_TYPE(32)	NULL

VERSIONS table

The VERSIONS table contains the version metadata. The values include a name, owner, status (public or private), state ID, and description.

VERSIONS

Name	Data_Type	Null?
name	SE_STRING_TYPE(32)	NOT NULL
Owner	SE_STRING_TYPE(32)	NOT NULL
Status	SE_INTEGER_TYPE	NOT NULL
State_id	SE_INTEGER_TYPE	NOT NULL

VERSIONS (continued)

Name	Data_Type	Null?
Description	SE_STRING_TYPE(65)	NULL
Parent_name	SE_STRING_TYPE(64)	NULL
Parent_owner	SE_STRING_TYPE(32)	NULL
Creation_time	SE_DATE_TYPE	NOT NULL

STATES table

The STATES table contains the state metadata. The values include a state ID, owner, creation and closing time, state ID of the parent state, and lineage information.

STATES

Name	Data_Type	Null?
state_id	SE_INTEGER_TYPE	NOT NULL
owner	SE_STRING_TYPE(32)	NOT NULL
creation_time	SE_DATE_TYPE	NOT NULL
closing_time	SE_DATE_TYPE	NULL
parent_state_id	SE_INTEGER_TYPE	NOT NULL
lineage_length	SE_INTEGER_TYPE	NOT NULL
Lineage	SE_BLOB_TYPE	NULL

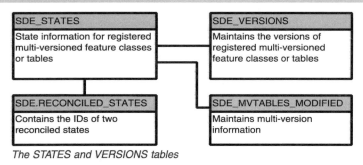

The STATES and VERSIONS tables

MVTABLES_MODIFIED table

The MVTABLES_MODIFIED table contains the state and table IDs modified in a given state.

MVTABLES_MODIFIED

Name	Data_Type	Null?
state_id	SE_INTEGER_TYPE	NOTNULL
registration_id	SE_INTEGER_TYPE	NOTNULL

RECONCILED_STATES table

The RECONCILED_STATES table contains the IDs for two reconciled states.

RECONCILED_STATES

Name	Data_Type	Null?
first_state_id	SE_INTEGER_TYPE	NOTNULL
second_state_id	SE_INTEGER_TYPE	NOTNULL

METADATA table

The METADATA table contains ArcSDE metadata.

METADATA

Name	Data_Type	Null?
record_id	SE_INTEGER_TYPE	NOTNULL
object_name	SE_STRING_TYPE(32)	NOTNULL
object_owner	SE_STRING_TYPE(32)	NOTNULL
object_type	SE_INTEGER_TYPE	NOTNULL
class_name	SE_STRING_TYPE(32)	NULL
property	SE_STRING_TYPE(32)	NULL
prop_value	SE_STRING_TYPE(255)	NULL
description	SE_STRING_TYPE(65)	NULL
creation_date	SE_DATE_TYPE	NOTNULL

LOCATORS table

The LOCATORS table stores information about locator objects.

LOCATORS

Name	Data_Type	Null?
locator_id	SE_INTEGER_TYPE	NOTNULL
name	SE_STRING_TYPE(32)	NOTNULL
owner	SE_STRING_TYPE(32)	NOTNULL
category	SE_STRING_TYPE(32)	NOTNULL
type	SE_INTEGER_TYPE	NOTNULL
description	SE_STRING_TYPE(64)	NULL

Geodatabase system tables

GDB_ANNOSYMBOLS table

The GDB_ANNOSYMBOLS table contains feature class annotation. The values include annosymbol ID and the annotation string.

GDB_ANNOSYMBOLS

Name	Data_Type	Null?
id	SE_INTEGER_TYPE	NOT NULL
symbol	SE_BLOB_TYPE	NULL

GDB_ATTRRULES table

The GDB_ATTRRULES table contains the rules for each attribute domain.

GDB_ATTRRULES

Name	Data_Type	Null?
ruleid	SE_INTEGER_TYPE	NOT NULL
subtype	SE_INTEGER_TYPE	NOT NULL
fieldname	SE_STRING_TYPE(32)	NOT NULL
domainname	SE_STRING_TYPE(160)	NOT NULL

GDB_CODEDDOMAINS table

The GDB_CODEDDOMAINS table contains coded values for each domain.

GDB_CODEDDOMAINS

Name	Data_Type	Null?
domainid	SE_INTEGER_TYPE	NOT NULL
codedvalues	SE_BLOB_TYPE	NOT NULL

GDB_DEFAULTVALUES table

The GDB_DEFAULTVALUES table contains the default values for the subtypes of each object class.

GDB_DEFAULTVALUES

Name	Data_Type	Null?
classid	SE_INTEGER_TYPE	NOT NULL
fieldname	SE_STRING_TYPE(32)	NOT NULL
subtype	SE_INTEGER_TYPE	NOT NULL
defaultstring	SE_STRING_TYPE(160)	NULL
defaultnumber	SE_STRING_TYPE(32)	NULL

GDB_DOMAINS table

The GDB_DOMAINS table contains the attribute constraints associated with attribute rules of the GDB_ATTRRULES table.

GDB_DOMAINS

Name	Data_Type	Null?
id	SE_INTEGER_TYPE	NOT NULL
owner	SE_STRING_TYPE(32)	NOT NULL
domainname	SE_STRING_TYPE(160)	NOT NULL
description	SE_STRING_TYPE(160)	NULL
domaintype	SE_INTEGER_TYPE	NOT NULL
fieldtype	SE_INTEGER_TYPE	NOT NULL
mergepolicy	SE_INTEGER_TYPE	NOT NULL
splitpolicy	SE_INTEGER_TYPE	NOT NULL

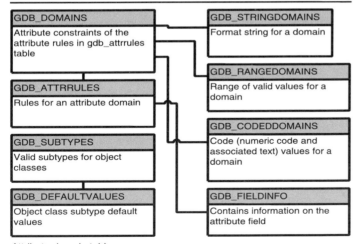

Attribute domain tables

GDB_EDGECONNRULES table

The GDB_EDGECONNRULES table contains the edge connectivity rules. Edge connectivity rules together with junction rules function to define the geometric networks stored in the gdb_geonetwork table.

GDB_EDGECONNRULES

Name	Data_Type	Null?
Ruleid	SE_INTEGER_TYPE	NOT NULL
Fromclassid	SE_INTEGER_TYPE	NOT NULL
Fromsubtype	SE_INTEGER_TYPE	NOT NULL
Toclassid	SE_INTEGER_TYPE	NOT NULL
Tosubtype	SE_INTEGER_TYPE	NOT NULL
Junctions	SE_BLOB_TYPE	NOT NULL

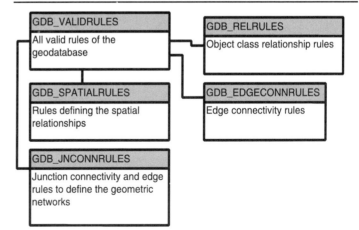

The geometric network edge/junction rules

GDB_FEATURECLASSES table

The GDB_FEATURECLASSES table contains the feature classes.

GDB_FEATURECLASSES

Name	Data_Type	Null?
Objectclassid	SE_INTEGER_TYPE	NOT NULL
featuretype	SE_INTEGER_TYPE	NOT NULL
geometrytype	SE_INTEGER_TYPE	NOT NULL
shapefield	SE_STRING_TYPE(32)	NOT NULL
geomnetworkid	SE_INTEGER_TYPE	NULL
graphid	SE_INTEGER_TYPE	NULL

GDB_FEATUREDATASET table

The GDB_FEATUREDATASET table contains the feature datasets. A feature dataset is a grouping of feature classes.

GDB_FEATUREDATASET

Name	Data_Type	Null?
id	SE_INTEGER_TYPE	NOT NULL
owner	SE_STRING_TYPE(32)	NOT NULL
name	SE_STRING_TYPE(255)	NOT NULL
srid	SE_INTEGER_TYPE	NOT NULL
databasename	SE_STRING_TYPE(32)	NULL

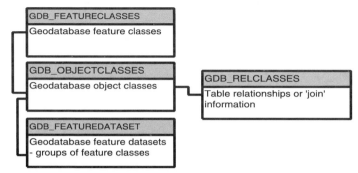

The feature/object class tables

GDB_FIELDINFO table

The GDB_FIELDINFO table contains the field name, default domain names values, default string, and number values for each attribute field associated with a feature class.

GDB_FIELDINFO

Name	Data_Type	Null?
classid	SE_INTEGER_TYPE	NOT NULL
fieldname	SE_STRING_TYPE(160)	NOT NULL
aliasname	SE_STRING_TYPE(160)	NULL
modelname	SE_STRING_TYPE(160)	NULL
defaultdomainname	SE_STRING_TYPE(160)	NULL
defaultvaluestring	SE_STRING_TYPE(160)	NULL
defaultvaluenumber	SE_DOUBLE_TYPE(38,8)	NULL
isrequired	SE_INTEGER_TYPE	NOT NULL
issubtypefixed	SE_INTEGER_TYPE	NOT NULL
iseditable	SE_STRING_TYPE(32)	NOT NULL

GDB_GEOMNETWORKS table

The GDB_GEOMNETWORKS table contains the geometric networks of a feature dataset.

GDB_GEOMNETWORKS

Name	Data_Type	Null?
id	SE_INTEGER_TYPE	NOT NULL
owner	SE_STRING_TYPE(32)	NOT NULL
name	SE_STRING_TYPE(160)	NOT NULL
networktype	SE_INTEGER_TYPE	NOT NULL
datasetid	SE_INTEGER_TYPE	NOT NULL
databasename	SE_STRING_TYPE(32)	NULL

GDB_JNCONNRULES table

The GDB_JNCONNRULES table contains the junction connectivity rules. Junction connectivity rules together with edges rules function to define the geometric networks stored in the GDB_GEOMNETWORKS table.

GDB_JNCONNRULES

Name	Data_Type	Null?
ruleid	SE_INTEGER_TYPE	NOT NULL
edgeclassid	SE_INTEGER_TYPE	NOT NULL
edgesubtype	SE_INTEGER_TYPE	NOT NULL
edgemincard	SE_INTEGER_TYPE	NOT NULL
edgemaxcard	SE_INTEGER_TYPE	NOT NULL
junctionclassid	SE_INTEGER_TYPE	NOT NULL
junctionsubtype	SE_INTEGER_TYPE	NOT NULL
junctionmincard	SE_INTEGER_TYPE	NOT NULL
junctionmaxcard	SE_INTEGER_TYPE	NOT NULL

GDB_NETCLASSES table

The GDB_NETCLASSES table contains the network classes of the geometric networks.

GDB_NETCLASSES

Name	Data_Type	Null?
classid	SE_INTEGER_TYPE	NOT NULL
networkid	SE_INTEGER_TYPE	NOT NULL
enabledfield	SE_STRING_TYPE(32)	NULL
ancillaryrole	SE_INTEGER_TYPE	NULL
ancillaryfield	SE_STRING_TYPE(32)	NULL

GDB_NETWEIGHTS table

The GDB_NETWEIGHTS table contains the network weights of the geometric networks.

GDB_NETWEIGHTS

Name	Data_Type	Null?
oid	SE_INTEGER	NOT NULL
networkid	SE_INTEGER	NOT NULL
name	SE_STRING	NOT NULL
weightid	SE_INTEGER	NOT NULL
weighttype	SE_INTEGER	NOT NULL
bitgatesize	SE_INTEGER	NULL

GDB_NETWEIGHTASOCS table

The GDB_NETWEIGHTASOCS table contains the association between the network classes and the network weights of the geometric networks.

GDB_NETWEIGHTASOCS

Name	Data_Type	Null?
networkid	SE_INTEGER_TYPE	NOT NULL
weightid	SE_INTEGER_TYPE	NOT NULL
tablename	SE_STRING_TYPE(160)	NOT NULL
fieldname	SE_STRING_TYPE(32)	NULL

GDB_NETWORKS table

The GDB_NETWORKS table contains the logical networks.

GDB_NETWORKS

Name	Data_Type	Null?
id	SE_INTEGER_TYPE	NOT NULL
owner	SE_STRING_TYPE(32)	NOT NULL
name	SE_STRING_TYPE(160)	NOT NULL
networktype	SE_INTEGER_TYPE	NOT NULL
indextype	SE_INTEGER_TYPE	NOT NULL
normalized	SE_INTEGER_TYPE	NOT NULL
databasename	SE_STRING_TYPE(32)	NULL

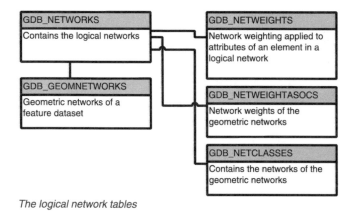

The logical network tables

GDB_OBJECTCLASSES table

The GDB_OBJECTCLASSES table contains all of the object classes in the geodatabase, which includes the feature classes, relationship classes, business tables, and columns.

GDB_OBJECTCLASSES

Name	Data_Type	Null?
id	SE_INTEGER_TYPE	NOT NULL
owner	SE_STRING_TYPE(32)	NOT NULL
name	SE_STRING_TYPE(160)	NOT NULL
aliasname	SE_STRING_TYPE(160)	NULL
modelname	SE_STRING_TYPE(160)	NULL
clsid	SE_STRING_TYPE(38)	NOT NULL
extclsid	SE_STRING_TYPE(38)	NULL
extprops	SE_BLOB_TYPE	NULL
subtypefield	SE_STRING_TYPE(32)	NULL
datasetid	SE_INTEGER_TYPE	NULL

GDB_RANGEDOMAINS table

The GDB_RANGEDOMAINS table contains the range of possible values allowed in a domain.

GDB_RANGEDOMAINS

Name	Data_Type	Null?
domainid	SE_INTEGER_TYPE	NOT NULL
minvalue	SE_DOUBLE_TYPE(38,8)	NOT NULL
maxvalue	SE_DOUBLE_TYPE(38,8)	NOT NULL

GDB_RELCLASSES table

The GDB_RELCLASSES table contains the table relationships required by the geodatabase.

GDB_RELCLASSES

Name	Data_Type	Null?
id	SE_INTEGER_TYPE	NOT NULL
owner	SE_STRING_TYPE(32)	NOT NULL
name	SE_STRING_TYPE(160)	NOT NULL
originclassid	SE_INTEGER_TYPE	NOT NULL
destclassid	SE_INTEGER_TYPE	NOT NULL
forwardlabel	SE_STRING_TYPE(32)	NULL
backwardlabel	SE_STRING_TYPE(32)	NULL
cardinality	SE_INTEGER_TYPE	NOT NULL
notification	SE_INTEGER_TYPE	NOT NULL
iscomposite	SE_INTEGER_TYPE	NOT NULL
isattributed	SE_INTEGER_TYPE	NOT NULL
originprimarykey	SE_STRING_TYPE(32)	NOT NULL
destprimarykey	SE_STRING_TYPE(32)	NOT NULL
originforeignkey	SE_STRING_TYPE(32)	NOT NULL
destforeignkey	SE_STRING_TYPE(32)	NOT NULL
datasetid	SE_INTEGER_TYPE	NULL
databasename	SE_STRING_TYPE(32)	NULL

GDB_RELEASE table

The GDB_RELEASE table stores geodatabase version release information as a single record.

GDB_RELEASE

Name	Data_Type	Null?
major	SE_INTEGER_TYPE	NOT NULL
minor	SE_INTEGER_TYPE	NOT NULL
bugfix	SE_INTEGER_TYPE	NOT NULL

GDB_RELRULES table

The GDB_RELRULES table contains the object class relationship rules.

GDB_RELRULES

Name	Data_Type	Null?
ruleid	SE_INTEGER_TYPE	NOT NULL
originsubtype	SE_INTEGER_TYPE	NOT NULL
originmincard	SE_INTEGER_TYPE	NOT NULL
originmaxcard	SE_INTEGER_TYPE	NOT NULL
destsubtype	SE_INTEGER_TYPE	NOT NULL
destmincard	SE_INTEGER_TYPE	NOT NULL
destmaxcard	SE_INTEGER_TYPE	NOT NULL

GDB_SPATIALRULES table

The GDB_SPATIALRULES table contains the spatial rules of the geodatabase. Such rules determine which spatial relationships are permitted.

GDB_SPATIALRULES

Name	Data_Type	Null?
rruleid	SE_INTEGER_TYPE	NOT NULL
subtype	SE_INTEGER_TYPE	NOT NULL
spatialrel	SE_INTEGER_TYPE	NOT NULL
distance	SE_DOUBLE_TYPE(38,8)	NOT NULL
relclassid	SE_INTEGER_TYPE	NOT NULL
relsubtype	SE_INTEGER_TYPE	NOT NULL

GDB_STRINGDOMAINS table

The GDB_STRINGDOMAINS table stores a domain's format string.

GDB_STRINGDOMAINS

Name	Data_Type	Null?
domainid	SE_INTEGER_TYPE	NOT NULL
format	SE_STRING_TYPE(32)	NOT NULL

GDB_SUBTYPES table

The GDB_SUBTYPES table contains the valid subtypes of the geodatabase object classes.

GDB_SUBTYPES

Name	Data_Type	Null?
id	SE_INTEGER_TYPE	NOT NULL
classid	SE_INTEGER_TYPE	NOT NULL
subtypecode	SE_INTEGER_TYPE	NOT NULL
subtypename	SE_STRING_TYPE(160)	NOT NULL

GDB_USERMETADATA table

The GDB_USERMETADATA table stores user metadata for all parts of the geodatabase including object classes, feature classes, feature datasets, logical networks, and relationship classes.

GDB_USERMETADATA

Name	Data_Type	Null?
id	SE_INTEGER_TYPE	NOT NULL
owner	SE_STRING_TYPE(32)	NOT NULL
name	SE_STRING_TYPE(160)	NOT NULL
datasettype	SE_INTEGER_TYPE	NOT NULL
xml	SE_BLOB_TYPE	NOT NULL
databasename	SE_STRING_TYPE(32)	NULL

GDB_VALIDRULES table

The GDB_VALIDRULES table contains all the valid rules of the geodatabase, which includes the attribute rules, edge connectivity rules, junction connectivity rules, relationship rules, and spatial rules.

GDB_VALIDRULES

Name	Data_Type	Null?
id	SE_INTEGER_TYPE	NOT NULL
ruletype	SE_INTEGER_TYPE	NOT NULL
classid	SE_INTEGER_TYPE	NOT NULL
rulecategory	SE_INTEGER_TYPE	NOT NULL
helpstring	SE_STRING_TYPE(160)	NULL

Appendix C: ArcSDE table definitions

This appendix lists the ArcSDE tables that a user can create, and that should be included within your existing backup arrangements. With the exception of the business table, these tables should only be accessed through the application interface provided either by ArcInfo or an ArcSDE C API program. Direct access to the nonbusiness tables via the SQL interface is not supported.

Business tables

The business table is an existing RDBMS table that ArcSDE spatially enables by adding a shape column. A spatial column is also known as a "layer", and information about each layer is maintained in the LAYERS table.

The data type of the shape column varies depending on the implementation of ArcSDE.

Binary schema implementation

With ArcSDE 8, most implementations employ the binary schema. Under this implementation, the integer shape column contains feature identifiers that uniquely reference the shape data. The feature ID joins the business table with the associated ArcSDE-managed feature and spatial index tables.

A trigger is defined on the spatially enabled business table to maintain the relationship between records in the business table and the feature table. The trigger is:

```
TRIGGER  SPCOL_DEL_CASCADE_<layer>
AFTER  DELETE  OR  UPDATE  OF  <SPATIAL_COL>  ON
business_table
    IF  DELETING  THEN
        DELETE  FROM  F<layer>
        WHERE  F<layer>.fid  =  old.<SPATIAL_COL>

        DELETE  FROM  S<layer>
        WHERE  S<layer>.fid  =  old.<SPATIAL_COL>


    IF  UPDATING  AND  new.<SPATIAL_COL>  IS  NULL  THEN
        DELETE  FROM  F<layer>
            WHERE  F<layer>.fid  =  old.<SPATIAL_COL>

        DELETE  FROM  S<layer>
            WHERE  S<layer>.fid  =  old.<SPATIAL_COL>


    IF  UPDATING  AND  new.<SPATIAL_COL>  !=
                        old.<SPATIAL_COL>  THEN
      raise_application_error

      (-20013,'Invalid  update  of  SDE  Spatial
      Column.')
```

Feature table

Under the binary schema implementation, the feature table stores the geometric shapes for each feature. This table is identified by the spatial column layer number using the name F<layer_id>.

The relationship between the business table and the feature table is managed through the Feature ID, or FID. This key, which is maintained by ArcSDE, is unique for the spatial column.

F<layer_id>

NAME	DATA_TYPE	NULL?
Fid	SE_INTEGER_TYPE	NOT NULL
numofpts	SE_INTEGER_TYPE	NOT NULL
entity	SE_SMALLINT_TYPE	NOT NULL
eminx	SE_FLOAT_TYPE(64)	NOT NULL
eminy	SE_FLOAT_TYPE(64)	NOT NULL
emaxx	SE_FLOAT_TYPE(64)	NOT NULL
emaxy	SE_FLOAT_TYPE(64)	NOT NULL
eminz	SE_FLOAT_TYPE(64)	NULL
emaxz	SE_FLOAT_TYPE(64)	NULL
min_measure	SE_FLOAT_TYPE(64)	NULL
max_measure	SE_FLOAT_TYPE(64)	NULL
area	SE_FLOAT_TYPE(64)	NOT NULL
len	SE_FLOAT_TYPE(64)	NOT NULL
points	SE_BLOB_TYPE	NULL

The feature table stores the shape geometry and has several additional columns to support ArcSDE query processing.

For storing the geometry:

- points (SE_BLOB)—contains the byte stream of point coordinates that define the shape's geometry

For query processing:

- area (SE_FLOAT_TYPE)—the area of the shape
- len (SE_FLOAT_TYPE)—the length or perimeter of the shape
- eminx, eminy, emaxx, emaxy (SE_FLOAT_TYPE)—the envelope of the shape
- eminz (SE_FLOAT_TYPE)—the minimum z-value in the shape
- emaxz (SE_FLOAT_TYPE)—the maximum z-value in the shape
- min_measure (SE_FLOAT_TYPE)—the minimum measure value in the shape
- max_measure (SE_FLOAT_TYPE)—the maximum measure value in the shape

For internal ArcSDE use:

- fid (SE_INTEGER_TYPE)—contains the unique ID that joins the feature table to the business table
- entity (SE_INTEGER_TYPE)—the type of geometric feature stored in the shape column (e.g., point, line string)
- numofpts (SE_INTEGER_TYPE)—the number of points defining the shape

As shapes are inserted or updated, the extents, numofpts, and so on are recalculated automatically. The points column contains the coordinate array for the shape in a compressed integer format. The binary layout of this data is discussed in the *ArcSDE Developer Help* located in the SDEHOME\documentation directory.

Spatial index table

The spatial index of the binary implementation is the spatial index table. It stores references to shapes based on a simple, regular grid. This table is identified by the spatial column layer number using the name S<layer_id>.

The spatial index contains an entry for each shape and grid cell combination. A feature that crosses into three grid cells has three entries in the table. When a spatial query is performed, the grid cells within the search area are identified and used to return a list of candidate shapes.

- sp_fid (SE_INTEGER_TYPE)—contains the ID that joins the spatial index table to the feature table
- gx, gy (SE_INTEGER_TYPE)—the grid cell coordinate
- eminx, eminy, emaxx, emaxy (SE_INTEGER_TYPE)—the envelope of the shape

S<layer_id>

NAME	DATA TYPE	NULL?
sp_fid	SE_INTEGER_TYPE	NOT NULL
gx	SE_INTEGER_TYPE	NOT NULL
gy	SE_INTEGER_TYPE	NOT NULL
eminx	SE_INTEGER_TYPE	NOT NULL
eminy	SE_INTEGER_TYPE	NOT NULL
emaxx	SE_INTEGER_TYPE	NOT NULL
emaxy	SE_INTEGER_TYPE	NOT NULL

Normalized schema

In the normalized schema, the coordinate values for a shape are stored as individual numeric data types in a separate geometry table. Access from a business table to a shape is through a foreign key—the Geometry ID, or GID.

The geometry table has at least six columns: GID, ETYPE, ESEQ, SEQ, and two coordinate values. The shape type (point, line string, or polygon) is stored as an ETYPE value. The ETYPE is either 1 (point), 2 (line string), or 3 (polygon). A normalized representation might not store all of a shape's coordinates in a single row in the geometry table. To accommodate shapes with a large number of values, the geometry is represented by multiple rows. The element sequence value, ESEQ, identifies multiple parts within a shape. Rows that represent a single part are listed by a sequence (SEQ) value so that rows are returned in the proper order.

The tables below illustrate the relationship between a business table and its geometry table in the normalized geometry representation. Any number of coordinate pairs are allowed for a given table. In this example, two coordinate pairs are stored for each row in the geometry table.

<GEOMETRY TABLE >

GID	ETYPE	ESEQ	SEQ	X1	Y1	X2	Y2
1	3	1	1	10.00	10.00	10.00	15.00
1	3	1	2	10.00	15.00	15.00	15.00
1	3	1	3	15.00	15.00	15.00	10.00
1	3	1	4	15.00	10.00	10.00	10.00
2	3	1	1	100.00	100.00	100.00	50.00
2	3	1	2	100.00	150.00	150.00	50.00
2	3	1	3	150.00	150.00	150.00	00.00
2	3	1	4	150.00	100.00	100.00	00.00
2	3	2	1	70.00	90.00	75.00	90.00
...	...	...	...	...	...	...	...

A geometry table with two shapes. The second shape has more than one part.

<BUSINESS TABLE>

Feature-ID	Column1	Column2	GeometryID
101			1
102			2
103			3
...			...

A business table with GIDs

Spatial types and functions schema

Some of the implementations of ArcSDE employ the latest object-relation technology. Instead of using a separate table to store the shapes, the spatial types and functions schema stores them directly in the shape column. Under this implementation, the shape column is an abstract data type (ADT).

The ArcSDE spatial types and functions implementation includes seven of the ADTs defined by OpenGIS® RFP-1. Those data types are point, line string, polygon, multipoint, multi-line string, multipolygon, and geometry.

The database administrator normally runs a program that adds these ADTs and a number of spatial functions to a database. After the ADTs and functions have been added, the database becomes "spatially enabled". Users may now create tables that include columns whose types are of the seven spatial ADTs listed above. As a bonus the spatial types and functions allow users to perform spatial queries using the SQL interface provided by the RDBMS vendor.

Logical network tables

The logical network tables provide connectivity and flow direction information between elements, the junctions and edges, in a network.

The N_*_EDESC table contains a description of the edges within a network.

N_*_EDESC

Name	Data_Type	Null?
oid	SE_INTEGER_TYPE	NOTNULL
pagenumber	SE_INTEGER_TYPE	NOTNULL
pageblob	SE_BLOB_TYPE	NULL

The N_*_ESTATUS table contains the status of each element including its deleted state and disabled state.

N_*_ESTATUS

Name	Data_Type	Null?
oid	SE_INTEGER_TYPE	NOTNULL
pagenumber	SE_INTEGER_TYPE	NOTNULL
pageblob	SE_BLOB_TYPE	NULL

The N_*_ETOPO table contains the edge topology.

N_*_ETOPO

Name	Data_Type	Null?
oid	SE_INTEGER_TYPE	NOTNULL
pagenumber	SE_INTEGER_TYPE	NOTNULL
pageblob	SE_BLOB_TYPE	NULL

The N_*_FLODIR table contains the flow direction.

N_*_FLODIR

Name	Data_Type	Null?
oid	SE_INTEGER_TYPE	NOTNULL
pagenumber	SE_INTEGER_TYPE	NOTNULL
pageblob	SE_BLOB_TYPE	NULL

The N_*_JDESC table contains a description of the junctions of a network.

N_*_JDESC

Name	Data_Type	Null?
oid	SE_INTEGER_TYPE	NOTNULL
pagenumber	SE_INTEGER_TYPE	NOTNULL
pageblob	SE_BLOB_TYPE	NULL

The N_*_JSTATUS table contains the status of each element including its deleted state and disabled state.

N_*_JSTATUS

Name	Data_Type	Null?
oid	SE_INTEGER_TYPE	NOT NULL
pagenumber	SE_INTEGER_TYPE	NOT NULL
pageblob	SE_BLOB_TYPE	NULL

The N_*_JTOPO table contains the junction topology.

N_*_JTOPO

Name	Data_Type	Null?
oid	SE_INTEGER_TYPE	NOT NULL
pagenumber	SE_INTEGER_TYPE	NOT NULL
pageblob	SE_BLOB_TYPE	NULL

The N_*_JTOPO2 table contains the overflow junction topology.

N_*_JTOPO2

Name	Data_Type	Null?
oid	SE_INTEGER_TYPE	NOT NULL
pagenumber	SE_INTEGER_TYPE	NOT NULL
pageblob	SE_BLOB_TYPE	NULL

The N_*_PROPS table contains the network properties including number of junctions, edges, and turns.

N_*_PROPS

Name	Data_Type	Null?
propertyid	SE_INTEGER_TYPE	NULL
propertyname	SE_STRING_TYPE(255)	NULL
propertyvalue	SE_INTEGER_TYPE	NULL

The N_*_E* table contains all of the network edge weights.

N_*_E*

Name	Data_Type	Null?
oid	SE_INTEGER_TYPE	NOT NULL
name	SE_STRING_TYPE	NULL
internalid	SE_INTEGER_TYPE	NULL
weighttype	SE_INTEGER_TYPE	NULL
maxvalue	SE_DOUBLE_TYPE(38,8)	NULL
minvalue	SE_DOUBLE_TYPE(38,8)	NULL

The N_*_J* table contains all of the network junction weights.

N_*_J*

Name	Data_Type	Null?
oid	SE_INTEGER_TYPE	NOT NULL
name	SE_STRING_TYPE	NULL
internalid	SE_INTEGER_TYPE	NULL
weighttype	SE_INTEGER_TYPE	NULL
maxvalue	SE_DOUBLE_TYPE(38,8)	NULL
minvalue	SE_DOUBLE_TYPE(38,8)	NULL

Log file tables

The SDE_LOGFILES table contains the log file metadata. The values include a log file name and ID, the registration ID, flags, and session information.

SDE_LOGFILES

Name	Data_Type	Null?
logfile_name	SE_STRING_TYPE(256)	NOT NULL
logfile_id	SE_INTEGER_TYPE	NOT NULL
logfile_data_id	SE_INTEGER_TYPE	NOT NULL
registration_id	SE_INTEGER_TYPE	NOT NULL
flags	SE_INTEGER_TYPE	NOT NULL
session_tag	SE_INTEGER_TYPE	NOT NULL

The SDE_LOGFILE_DATA table contains the list of business table records that are part of each log.

SDE_LOGFILE_DATA

Name	Data_Type	Null?
logfile_data_id	SE_INTEGER_TYPE	NOT NULL
sde_row_id	SE_INTEGER_TYPE	NOT NULL

Version tables

The version tables store information about the changes (additions or deletions) that are made to a versioned business table.

The A<registration_ID> table (or the "adds" table) stores the records added to each state in a versioned business table.

A<registration_ID>

Name	Data_Type	Null?
User-defined column names	User-defined data types	
.	.	
.	.	
.	.	
sde_state_id	SE_INTEGER_TYPE	NOT NULL

The D<registration_ID> table (or the "deletes" table) conversely, stores the records deleted from each state in a versioned business table.

D<registration_ID>

Name	Data_Type	Null?
sde_state_id	SE_INTEGER_TYPE	NOT NULL
sde_row_id	SE_INTEGER_TYPE	NOT NULL
Deleted_at	SE_INTEGER_TYPE	NOT NULL

Raster tables

ArcSDE stores images in three raster tables. The raster blocks table, SDE_BLK_<raster_column_ID>, stores the actual image data for each band of the image. The raster band table, SDE_BND_<raster_column_ID>, stores metadata about the bands of the image. The raster description table, SDE_RAS_<raster_column_ID>, stores the description of the images within a raster column. The raster column that is added to the business table stores the raster ID, which joins the business table to the three raster tables.

The raster blocks table, SDE_BLK_<raster_column_ID>, stores the image tiles.

SDE_BLK_<raster_column_ID>

Name	Data_Type	Null?
rasterband_id	SE_INTEGER_TYPE	NOT NULL
rrd_factor	SE_INTEGER_TYPE	NOT NULL
row_nbr	SE_INTEGER_TYPE	NOT NULL
col_nbr	SE_INTEGER_TYPE	NOT NULL
block_data	SE_BLOB_TYPE	NOT NULL

The raster description table, SDE_RAS_<raster_column_ID>, stores the description of the images stored in a raster column.

SDE_RAS_<raster_column_ID>

Name	Data_Type	Null?
raster_id	SE_INTEGER_TYPE	NOT NULL
description	SE_STRING_TYPE(65)	NULL

The raster band table, SDE_BND_<raster_column_ID>, stores information about the bands of the images. Among other things this table stores is the width and height of the band tiles, the pixel type, and pixel depth.

SDE_BND_<raster_column_ID>

NAME	DATA TYPE	NULL?
rasterband_id	SE_INTEGER_TYPE	NOT NULL
sequence_nbr	SE_INTEGER_TYPE	NOT NULL
raster_id	SE_INTEGER_TYPE	NOT NULL
name	SE_STRING_TYPE(65)	NULL
band_flags	SE_INTEGER_TYPE	NOT NULL
band_width	SE_INTEGER_TYPE	NOT NULL
band_height	SE_INTEGER_TYPE	NOT NULL
band_types	SE_INTEGER_TYPE	NOT NULL
block_width	SE_INTEGER_TYPE	NOT NULL
block_height	SE_INTEGER_TYPE	NOT NULL
eminx	SE_FLOAT_TYPE(64)	NOT NULL
eminy	SE_FLOAT_TYPE(64)	NOT NULL
emaxx	SE_FLOAT_TYPE(64)	NOT NULL
emaxy	SE_FLOAT_TYPE(64)	NOT NULL
cdate	SE_FLOAT_TYPE(64)	NOT NULL
mdate	SE_FLOAT_TYPE(64)	NOT NULL
statistics	SE_BLOB_TYPE	NULL

Appendix D: ArcSDE command references

The administration commands allow the ArcSDE administrator, usually a database administrator, to manage and monitor the use of an ArcSDE service. This appendix describes these commands in detail, providing both the syntax and example usage.

Command listing

The command names begin with "sde" except for two, shpinfo and shp2sde. The names identify the command's functions. For example, sdetable works with tables, while sdeimport imports ArcSDE export files.

ArcSDE command	Description
cov2sde	Imports data from a coverage
sdeexport	Creates an ArcSDE export file
sdegroup	Uses tiles to group shapes into multipart shapes
sdeimport	Imports data from an ArcSDE export file
sdelayer	Administers feature classes (layers)
sdelocator	Administers locators
sdelog	Administers log files
sdemon	Manages the ArcSDE server
sderelease	Lists the ArcSDE server version or upgrades the server
sdeservice	Manages the ArcSDE service on Windows NT platforms
sdetable	Administers business tables
sde2cov	Converts an ArcSDE feature class (layer) to a coverage
sde2shp	Converts an ArcSDE feature class (layer) to a shapefile
sde2tbl	Converts an ArcSDE table to a dBASE®, INFO™, or ArcSDE table

ArcSDE command	Description (continued)
sdeversion	Manages versions and states
sdexinfo	Describes an ArcSDE export file
shpinfo	Reports information about a shapefile
shp2sde	Converts an ESRI® shapefile to an ArcSDE feature class (layer)
tbl2sde	Converts a dBASE, INFO, or ArcSDE table to an ArcSDE table

Command syntax

The administration commands use UNIX command syntax and notation according to the following conventions:

-letter	Specifies a command operation or option, for example, "-o" or "-a". Letters are both lowercase and uppercase.
<>	Required argument. Replace appropriately. For example, "-u <DB_User_name>" could become "-u av".
		Mutually exclusive arguments. Pick one from the list.
{ }	Used with "	" to specify a list of choices for an argument.
[]	Optional parameter.

Each command has "operations" and "options". An operation does a specific task related to the command and is specified with "-o <task>". For example, some of the sdetable command operations are:

```
sdetable  -o create
sdetable  -o delete
sdetable  -o truncate
sdetable  -o list
sdetable  -o describe
sdetable  -o create_index
sdetable  -o delete_index
```

Each operation has a set of options. Just like operations, options are specified by "-<letter>". The "-<letter>" used for a particular option is standard across all commands. For instance, the option to specify a service is always "-i". Sometimes a letter is used for two different types of options, but never in the same command. In sdelayer, the "-f" option defines the initial number of features and average points per feature. Other administration commands use "-f" to point to a file.

For each command's operation, there are mandatory and non-mandatory options.

```
sdelog  -o list -u <username> [-i <service>] [-q]
```

The example above has three options. Anything enclosed within "[ ]" isn't required. The username option is required, while service "[i]" and quiet "[q]" aren't. Sometimes an option marked optional is not truly optional. The most common occurrence is "[-p <DB_User_password>]". It is optional on the command line, but ArcSDE will query for the password if it is not given.

```
$ sdetable   -o delete -t test30 -u sde
Password:
```

Some options have a list of choices such as

```
shp2sde -o append [-a {none | all |
file=<file_name>}]
```

The "-a" option in this example allows you to choose how to execute the option. These elements are enclosed in curly brackets.

A few options have two or more parameters separated by commas. The most common is

```
-l <table,column>
```

which specifies a business table and column. Do not add spaces between the parameters.

```
-l parcels,feature
```

UNIX users should be careful with special characters such as "?". Depending on the UNIX shell version, you may need to use the appropriate quote character to use a special character. For example, you can use the "-?" operation with any administration command to get help. If you're using a C shell (rather than a

Bourne shell), you must use "\", which tells the shell to use the next character directly rather than as a special character. Therefore, in a C shell, you must use

```
$ sdetable -\?
```

In a Bourne shell, you can simply use

```
$ sdetable -?
```

Some commands include optional SQL query statements, or "where clauses", to limit the features retrieved from a table or log file. If this option is included, the query must be quoted (for example, "area < 1000"). If your RDBMS encloses character literals with single quotes, enclose the entire expression with double quotes (e.g., " state_code = 'CO' "). If your RDBMS encloses character literals with double quotes, enclose the entire expression with single quotes, for example, ' state_code = "CO" ' .

Getting help

You can list the usage, operations, and options for any ArcSDE
administration command with the "-h" or "-?" options.

```
$ sderelease -h


-?
-h


-o upgrade  [-p <DB_Admin_password>] [-N] [-q]
-o list     [-p <DB_Admin_password>] [-q]

Operations:
        Upgrade  Upgrade ArcSDE Server
        list     List installed ArcSDE release

Options:
        -N      No verification
        -o      Operation
        -p      ArcSDE administrator RDBMS password
        -q      Quiet
        -h      Prints usage and options
        -?      Prints usage and options
```

Working with ArcSDE services

You can specify a service in several ways. By default, the service is named in the SDEHOME/etc/services.sde file. However, you can override the service in the services.sde file in three ways:

- The SDEINSTANCE environment variable can be set to the name of a service.

  `setenv SDEINSTANCE esri_sde3`

- The sdemon command "-i <service>" option accepts the service name as its argument.

- The sdemon command "-H <sde_directory>" option specifies the home directory (normally one not specified by $SDEHOME) within which the etc/services.sde file contains the service name.

The "-i <service>" and "-H <sde_directory>" options are mutually exclusive and cannot be used together. Either of the options override the service specified in both the SDEINSTANCE variable and the SDEHOME\etc\services.sde file.

Either

`<service> is specified in the -i option`

or

`<service> is listed in the services.sde`
`file located in the home directory`
`specified by the -h <sde_directory> option.`

If neither of the above have been specified:

`The service is specified by the SDEINSTANCE`
`system variable.`

If no SDEINSTANCE variable exists:

`The service is specified in the SDEHOME/`
`etc/services.sde file.`

The above set of rules does not apply to the sdemon "-o start" operation. For this operation, you cannot directly name the service; it must be read from a services.sde file. Therefore, the "start" operation doesn't use the service specified in the SDEINSTANCE variable, nor is the "-i <service>" option available for this particular operation.

Administration commands and services

All administration commands, except sderelease, connect to the service through the giomgr process and are clients of the ArcSDE service.

For these commands the default service is "esri_sde". To operate on a service other than the default, you must set the SDEINSTANCE variable or include the "-i <service>" option on the administration command line.

`$ setenv SDEINSTANCE production`

`$ sdelayer -o list -u arcview -p mapobjects`

or

`$ sdelayer -o list -u arcview -p mapobjects`
`-i production`

The sderelease command behaves differently because it must be able to access the ArcSDE version information of the database while the giomgr process is not running.

For sderelease, the default service is "esri_sde" unless the SDEHOME variable is set; if the variable is set, the service is specified in the SDEHOME\etc\services.sde file. The sderelease command also requires you to enter the database administrator's password.

ArcSDE system environment variables

All of the administration commands are located in the bin directory under $SDEHOME or %SDEHOME%. Each program within the bin directory administers different parts of the ArcSDE installation. Be sure to set the $SDEHOME or %SDEHOME% environment variable and include $SDEHOME/bin or %SDEHOME%\bin in your system "path" variable. Once you add the bin directory to the PATH environment variable, you can execute the administration programs without the full file specification.

You can also set other environment variables. ArcSDE administration commands such as sdelayer and cov2sde often require you to specify the server, service, database, user, and password. You can avoid having to type these by defining environment variables. ▶

Setting ArcSDE system environment variables on UNIX

1. Using the appropriate UNIX shell syntax, set the SDEHOME variable to reflect the ArcSDE installation directory.

   In this example, ArcSDE is installed under "/disk1".

2. Print the current shell environment to confirm settings.

① *Bourne Shell:*　　$ SDEHOME=/disk1/sdeexe40
　　　　　　　　　　　$ export SDEHOME

　　C Shell:　　　　$ setenv SDEHOME /disk1/
　　　　　　　　　　　sdeexe40

② *Bourne Shell:*　　$ env
　　C Shell:　　　　$ printenv

Setting ArcSDE system environment variables on Windows NT

1. Click the Start menu, select Settings, and click Control Panel. Double-click Systems and click the Environment tab on the Systems Properties panel.

2. Type SDEHOME in the Variable input box and type the path to the ArcSDE installation in the Value input box.

3. Click Set and then click OK.

The supported variables are:

- SDESERVER—ArcSDE server

- SDEDATABASE—your database name (not required for some RDBMSs)

- SDEINSTANCE—ArcSDE service name

- SDEUSER—your username

- SDEPASSWORD—your password

You may override the environment variables by typing a different value on the command line. Normally, if you don't give your password, you are prompted for it. If the SDEPASSWORD environment variable is set, that value is used and you won't be prompted. Storing a password with the SDEPASSWORD environment variable is not secure.

Setting the ArcSDE-supported variables on UNIX and Windows NT

1. Set each supported variable using the appropriate UNIX shell syntax or use the MS–DOS "set" command.

2. As an example, try using the sdelayer command to describe a feature class (layer).

3. If these variables haven't been defined, you must use this alternative command syntax.

 Bourne Shell:
```
$ SDESERVER=cymru
$ export  SDESERVER

$ SDEINSTANCE=arcsde8
$ export  SDEINSTANCE
$ SDEUSER=sdeuser
$ export  SDEUSER

$ SDEPASSWORD=cymru
$ export  SDEPASSWORD
```

C Shell:
```
$ setenv  SDESERVER  cymru
$ setenv  SDEINSTANCE  arcsde8
$ setenv  SDEUSER  sdeuser
$ setenv  SDEPASSWORD  sdepswd
```

MS–DOS:
```
C:>\ set  SDESERVER  cymru
C:>\ set  SDEINSTANCE  arcsde8
C:>\ set  SDEUSER  sdeuser
C:>\ set  SDEPASSWORD  sdepswd
```

 `$ sdelayer -o describe -l cities,shape`

3 `$ sdelayer -o describe -l cities,shape -s cymru -i arcsde8 -u sdeuser -p sdepswd`

ArcSDE administration commands: cov2sde

This command converts ArcInfo data to ArcSDE feature classes.

Usage syntax

```
cov2sde   -h

cov2sde   -o create -l <table,column>
          [-V <version_name>] -f
          <cover,feature_cls>
          -g <grid_size>  [{-R <SRID> |
          [Spatial_Ref_Opts]}]
          [-r <anno_relate>] [-d <dissolve_item>]
          [-M <minimum_ID>]
          [-S <layer_description_str>]
          [-e <entity_mask>] [-v]
          [-a <{none | all | file=<file_name>}>]
          [-k <config_keyword>]
          [-c <commit_interval>]
          [-i <service>] [-s <server_name>]
          [-D <database>] -u <DB_User_name>
          [-p <DB_User_password>]

where Spatial_Ref_Opts is
          [-x <xoffset,yoffset,xyscale>]
          [-z <zoffset,zscale>]
          [-m <moffset,mscale>]
          [-G {<projection_ID> |
          file=<proj_file_name>}]

cov2sde   -o init -l <table,column> -f
          <cover,feature_cls>
          [-r <anno_relate>]
          [-d <dissolve_item>]
          [-a <{none | all | file=<file_name>}>]
          [-c <commit_interval>]
          [-i <service>] [-s <server_name>]
          [-D <database>] [-u <DB_User_name>
          [-p <DB_User_password>] [-v]

cov2sde   -o append -l <table,column>
          [-V <version_name>]
          -f <cover,feature_cls>
          [-r <anno_relate>]
          [-d <dissolve_item>] [-a <{none | all
          | file=<file_name>}>]
          [-c <commit_interval>]
          [-i <service>] [-s <server_name>]
          [-D <database>] -u <DB_User_name>
          [-p <DB_User_password>] [-v]
```

Operations

create	Creates a new ArcSDE feature class and imports features into the new feature class from the coverage feature class—an error is returned if the feature class already exists
init	Deletes all of the features of an existing feature class before importing new features from the coverage feature class
append	Adds features from the coverage to an existing feature class—the default

Options

-a   Attribute mode:

    none   Do not load any attributes—this is the default

    all   Load all attribute columns. If no attribute table exists for the feature class, one will be created. If one exists, then incoming schema must be union compatible with the existing table if the APPEND option is used.

    file=<file_name>

        File containing lines of the form <INFO_item> [SDE_column]. The INFO_item selects the column to be output; the SDE_column (optional) is the new column name to be specified.

-c   Commit rate (default: AUTOCOMMIT from $SDEHOME/etc/giomgr.defs)

-d   Dissolve item for Map LIBRARIAN layer only

-D   Database name

-e   Entity types allowed (npsla3+MA)

-f   Input feature class name from coverage, Map LIBRARIAN layer, or ArcStorm™ layer

-g   Map layer grid sizes (not used by ArcSDE for Informix)

-G   Projection specifier (default: coverage's projection if exists)
    <projection_ID> Projection ID

Options (continued)

    file=<proj_file_name>
        File containing projection description string

-h   Prints usage and options

-i   ArcSDE service name

-k   Layer configuration keyword (default: DEFAULTS)

-l   Map layer table and spatial column name

-m   Measure offset, measure scale

-M   Layer's minimum ID (default: 1)

-o   Operation

-p   ArcSDE user RDBMS password

-r   Annotation relate name to load anno and feature at the same time. Relate will be loaded from the INFO table <cover.REL>.

-R   Spatial reference ID (SRID)

-s   ArcSDE server hostname (default: localhost)

-S   Map layer description string

-u   ArcSDE user RDBMS username

-v   Verbose diagnostic output

-V   Version name. If specified, data is inserted into the version. Not allowed for the init operation

-x   xoffset, yoffset, xyscale (default: 0.0, 0.0, 1.0)

-z   zoffset, zscale (default: 0.0, 1.0)

-?   Prints usage and options (use "-\?" on C shell)

Discussion

Cov2sde won't load feature-associated annotation from Map LIBRARIAN layers. To load feature-associated annotation from Map LIBRARIAN, extract the data to a coverage and then import it.

Feature class to ArcSDE entity type mapping

Coverage feature class	ArcSDE entity type
point, node	point (p)
line	simple line, line (sl)
polygon	area (a)
region.<subclass>	multipart area (a+)
route.<subclass>	multipart lines with measures (slM+)
anno.<subclass>	point, line, simple line, ANNO (pslA)

If loading annotations with no subclass using the "-o create" operation, you must use the "-a none" option. You can also load annotations with no subclass into an existing feature class (layer) with the "-o append" or "-o init" operations.

Column names that contain a pound sign "#" or a dash "-" will have different names in the new ArcSDE feature class (layer) because these characters are converted to underscores. Although <cover># and <cover>-id will be different, cov2sde will automatically match these columns. If multiple coverages with the same items are imported, create only one feature class (layer) and then load all subsequent coverages with the "-o append" operation; the <cover># and <cover>-id items will be matched automatically.

The "- create" operation requires you to provide a spatial reference. You may use an existing spatial reference system by entering the SRID number. Valid SRID numbers may be obtained by querying the sde.spatial_references table.

You can also enter the spatial reference by supplying the information directly. Spatial reference information includes the x- and y-coordinate offsets, x- and y-coordinate system units, z-coordinate offset, z-coordinate system units, measures offset, measure system units and the coordinate reference system. If no false x,y and scale values are provided by the "-x" option, the extent of the coverage, ArcStorm™ library, or map library is used to calculate these values automatically. Note that the resulting feature class (layer) will have the highest attainable scale factor for that extent. If features that fall outside of the original coverage's extent are appended to the feature class (layer) with subsequent loading operations, they will be rejected.

Examples

1. Loading the regions from a coverage:

```
$ cov2sde -o create -l country,shape -f
country,region.cntry -a all -s tiffany -i
esri_av -u andy -p passwrd -g 20,0,0
```

```
ESRI SDE: Coverage to Layer Loading Utility Thu
Jan 15 13:24:08 1998
_____

Loading feature class/subclass "region.cntry"

from Coverage "country"

Imported 166 features into SDE country,shape from
coverage

country,region.cntry

Cov2SDE completed.
```

2. Loading polygons from an ArcStorm layer:

```
ESRI SDE: Coverage to Layer Loading Utility Wed
Aug  6 12:10:11 1997
_____

Loading feature class/subclass "polygon"

from ArcStorm layer "/ultra1/worldas/worldlib/
country"

Cov2SDE completed.
```

3. Loading lines from a coverage with feature-associated annotation:

First, establish a relate between the feature attribute table (in this case AAT) and the text attribute table (TAT). Save the relate to an INFO file named <cover>.rel:

```
Arc: relate add
Relation Name: cityrel
Table Identifier: cities.tatname
Database Name: info
```

```
INFO Item: cities-id
Relate Column: cities-id
Relate Type: linear
Relate Access: ro
Relation Name:
Arc: relate save cities.rel
1 Relates saved to file cities.rel
```

```
Arc: q
```

Specify the name of the relate with -r <relate>. Cov2sde will load the relate from the INFO file called <cover>.rel:

```
$ cov2sde -o create -l cities,feature -f
cities,point -r cityrel -g 20,0,0 -x -180,-
90,10000 -e pA -k WORLD -a all -s stout -u
world -p world

Loading feature class/subclass "point" from
Coverage "cities"


Imported 606 features into SDE cities,feature
from coverage cities,point

Cov2SDE completed.
```

4. Loading standalone annotation from an ArcStorm layer:

```
$ cov2sde -o create -l rivernames,feature -f
worldas.worldlib.rivers, anno.riv -g 20,0,0
-x -180,-90,10000 -e slA -k WORLD -a all -s
stout -u world -p world
```

```
ESRI SDE: Coverage to Layer Loading Utility Wed
Aug  6 12:10:11 1997
_____

Loading feature class/subclass "anno.riv"

from ArcStorm layer "/ultra1/worldas/worldlib/
rivers"

Cov2SDE completed.
```

5. Loading feature-associated annotation from an ArcStorm layer:

First, establish a relate between the feature attribute table (in this case PAT) and the text attribute table (TAT). Save the relate to an INFO file named <database>.<library>.<layer>.rel:

```
Arc: relate add

Relation Name: cityrel

Table Identifier: !cities.tatname

Database Name: info

INFO Item: cities-id

Relate Column: cities-id

Relate Type: linear

Relate Access: ro

Relation Name:

Arc: relate save worldas.worldlib.cities.rel

1 Relates saved to file
worldas.worldlib.cities.rel

Arc: q
```

Specify the name of the relate with -r <relate>. Cov2sde will load the relate from an INFO file called <database>.<library>.<layer>.rel:

```
$ cov2sde -o create -l cityname,shape -f
worldas.worldlib.cities,point -r cityrel -e
pA -g 20,0,0 -a all -u world -p world


ESRI SDE: Coverage to Layer Loading Utility Fri
Sep  5 11:10:31 1997
_____

Loading feature class/subclass "point"

from ArcStorm layer "/bevo4/andym/arcstorm/
worldas/worldlib/cities"

Cov2SDE completed.
```

6. Creating a multiversioned feature class (layer) from a polygon coverage:

```
$ sdeversion -o create -V version1 -S 0 -A
public -d 'Base version' -u andy -p andy -s
tiffany -i esri_av

ESRI SDE: Coverage to Layer Loading Utility Thu
Sep 23 11:22:49 1999
_____

Successfully created new version ANDY.version1:

Base version
_____
```

Version Name:	MARK.version1
Parent Version Name:	
State ID:	0
Access:	Public
Creation Time:	Thu Sep 23 11:22:49 1999

```
$ cov2sde -o create -l country,shape -f
country,polygon -a all -s tiffany -i
esri_av -u andy -p passwrd -g 20,0,0 -V
version1

ESRI SDE: Coverage to Layer Loading Utility Tue
Jun 15 13:24:08 1999
_____

Loading feature class/subclass "polygon"

from Coverage "country"

Imported 273 features into SDE country,shape from
coverage country,polygon

Cov2SDE completed.
```

ArcSDE administration commands: sdeexport

This command creates an ArcSDE export file.

Usage syntax

```
sdeexport -h
sdeexport [-o create] -l <table,column>
          [-V <version_name>]
          -f <{export_file | -}>
          [-O] [-w <"where_clause">]
          [-i <service>] [-s <server_name>]
          [-D <database>] -u <DB_User_name>
          [-p <DB_User_password>]
sdeexport -o create21 -l <table,column>
          [-V <version_name>]
          -f <{export_file | -}> [-O]
          [-w <"where_clause">] [-i <service>]
          [-s <server_name>]
          [-D <database>] -u <DB_User_name>
          [-p <DB_User_password>]
```

Operations

create	Creates export format file version 3.0.2 (default)—for backward compatibility
create21	Creates export format file for SDE 2.1

Options

-f	Export format filename. Export to standard output if set to "-".
-h	Prints usage and options
-i	ArcSDE service name
-l	Map layer table and spatial column name
-O	Export in spatial index order
-p	ArcSDE user RDBMS password
-s	ArcSDE server hostname (default: localhost)
-u	ArcSDE user RDBMS username
-V	Version name. If specified, use only the data that belongs to the version.
-w	SQL where clause
-?	Prints usage and options (use "-\?" on C shell)

ArcSDE administration commands: sdegroup

This command merges features using tiles.

Usage syntax

```
sdegroup    -h
sdegroup    -?
sdegroup    -o create -S <source_layer,spl_column>
            [-s <server_name>] -T <target_layer,
            spl_column> [-t <Tile_size>]
            -e <entity_type>
            [-a <{none | all | file=<file_name>}>]
            [-D <database>] [-c <commit_interval>]
            [-i <service>] [-k <config_keyword>]
            [-w <"where_clause">] -g <grid_size>
            -u <DB_User_name>
            [-p DB_User_password>] [-q]
sdegroup    -o init -S <source_layer,spl_column>
            [-s <server_name>]
            -T <target_layer,spl_column>
            [-t <Tile_size>] [-D <database>]
            [-c <commit_interval>] [-i <service>]
            [-a <{none | all | file=<file_name>}>]
            [-k <config_keyword>]
            [-w <"where_clause">]
            -u <DB_User_name>
            [-p <DB_User_password>] [-N] [-q]
sdegroup    -o append -S <source_layer,spl_column>
            [-s <server_name>]
            -T <target_layer,spl_column>
            [-t <Tile_size>] [-D <database>]
            [-c <commit_interval>][-i <service>]
            [-a <{none | all | file=<file_name>}>]
            [-k <config_keyword>]
            [-w <"where_clause">]
            -u <DB_User_name>
            [-p <DB_User_password>]
            [-N] [-q]
```

Operations

create	Creates a new ArcSDE layer and imports features into it from a source layer based on a grouping of shapes into a single feature
init	Deletes all features from an existing target layer before importing the grouped features from the source layer
append	Adds features from a source layer into any existing target layer

Options

-a	Attribute mode:
	none Do not load any attributes—default
	all Load all attribute columns. If no attribute table exists for the feature, one will be created. If one exists, then incoming schema must be union compatible with the existing table if the APPEND option is used.
	file=<file_name> File containing lines of the form <shape_column> [sde_column]. The shape_column selects the column to be output; the sde_column is the new name to be specified.
-c	Commit rate
-D	Database or data source name. Not supported by all RDBMSs.
-e	Entity types allowed (psla+). If your source layer has multiple shape types but you restrict the entity type to one shape type, only that shape type is copied to the target feature class. For example, if the source layer has lines and area shapes, but you use "-e a+", only area shapes will be grouped and written to the new layer.
	p Point shapes
	s Line (spaghetti) shapes
	l Simple line (line string) shapes
	a Area shapes
	+ Multipart shapes

Options (continued)

-g	Map layer grid sizes. Grid cell sizes or levels 2 and 3 are optional. Examples are "-g 200" or "-g 200,1000,4000".
-h	Prints usage and options
-i	ArcSDE service name
-k	Layer configuration keyword present in the SDEHOME/etc/dbtune.sde file. The storage parameters specific to the layer will be found under the specified keyword.
-N	No verification is performed—the operation begins immediately after being invoked
-o	Operation
-p	ArcSDE user RDBMS password
-q	Quiet; all titles and warnings are suppressed
-s	ArcSDE server hostname (default: localhost)
-S	Source layer and spatial column names. If you are not the owner of the table, you must qualify the table name as "owner.table".
-t	The size of the tiles (default size is 2)
-T	Target layer and spatial column names. If you are not the owner of the table, you must qualify the table name as "owner.table".
-u	ArcSDE user RDBMS username
-w	SQL where clause
-?	Prints usage and options (use "-\?" on C shell)

Discussion

The sdegroup command uses tiles to group shapes into new multipart shapes. Using sdegroup can improve performance and display speed by reducing the number of rows that must be fetched from the database. However, you will lose the attribute data except for the first feature found in each tile.

Use a common viewing or query area to determine the tile size. If clients usually want to see an area of 1,600 square miles (40 by 40 miles) on a feature class (layer) that's 40,000 square miles (200 by 200 miles), you might want to use a tile size of 40. This will group the original features into 25 new features. Remember to consider the unit of measure of the feature class (layer). If the feature class's (layer) unit of measure is feet, you would use 211,200 for the previous example.

Because you're reducing the number of features in the feature, you should increase the size of the spatial index grid cell sizes. How much depends on the size of the resulting grouped features.

To create a new feature class (layer) called target_cities from the original cities feature class, use the following command syntax:

```
$ sdegroup -o create -S cities,shape -T
target_cities,shape -t 1 -e p+ -g 20,0,0 -u
av -p mo -i esri_40
```

The tile size is one, and only points will be copied from the cities feature class (layer).

ArcSDE administration commands: sdeimport

This command imports data from an ArcSDE export file.

Usage syntax

```
sdeimport -h

sdeimport -o append -l <table,column>
          [-V <version_name>]
          -f <{export_file | -}> [-v]
          [-c <commit_interval>]
          [-i <service>] [-s <server_name>]
          [-D <database>] -u <DB_User_name>
          [-p <DB_User_password>]

sdeimport -o init -l <table,column>
          -f <{export_file | -}> [-v]
          [-c <commit_interval>]
          [-i <service>] [-s <server_name>]
          [-D <database>] -u <DB_User_name>
          [-p <DB_User_password>]

sdeimport -o create -l <table,column>
          [-V <version_name>]
          -f <{export_file | -}> [-v]
          [-t <storageType>]
          [-g <grid_size> ]
          [-M <minimum_ID>]
          [-k <config_keyword>]
          [-c <commit_interval>]
          [-i <service>] [-s <server_name>]
          [-D <database>] -u <DB_User_name>
          [-p <DB_User_password>]
```

Operations

append	Imports features into an existing layer (default)
init	Deletes all features of an existing layer before importing new features
create	Creates a new layer based on the definition stored in the export file and imports features into the new layer—an error is returned if the layer already exists

Options

-c	Commit rate (defaults to the AUTOCOMMIT value in the giomgr.defs file)
-D	Database or data source name. Not supported by all RDBMSs.
-f	Export format filename. If set to '-', import from standard input.
-g	Map layer grid sizes. Grid cell sizes for levels 2 and 3 are optional. Examples are "-g 200" or "-g 200,1000,4000".
-h	Prints usage and options
-i	ArcSDE service name
-k	Layer configuration keyword—used with the "create" operation only
-l	Map layers's table and spatial column names. If you are not the owner of the table, you must qualify the table name as "owner.table" and have insert privileges.
-M	Minimum feature ID. New shape IDs are assigned the larger of the minimum ID or the maximum assigned ID + one. Default is 1.
-o	Operation
-p	ArcSDE user RDBMS password
-s	ArcSDE server hostname (default: localhost)
-t	Storage type—allowed values are B (ArcSDE binary), N (normalized), W (well-known binary), or Q (SQL type)
-u	ArcSDE user RDBMS username

Options (continued)

v	Verbose option—reports records committed
-V	Version name. If specified, insert the data into the version. Not allowed for the init operation.
-?	Prints usage and options (use "-\?" on C shell)

ArcSDE administration commands: sdelayer

This command administers feature classes.

Usage syntax

```
sdelayer   -o add -l <table,column>
           -e <entity_mask> -g <grid_size>
           [{-R <SRID> | {Spatial_Ref_Opts]}]
           [-M <minimum_id>]
           [{-f <init_features,avg_points> | -k
           <config_keyword>}]
           [-E <{empty | calc
           |xmin,ymin,xmax,ymax}>]
           [-t <storage_type>]
           [-S <layer_description_str>]
           [-i <service>] [-s <server_name>]
           [-D <database>] -u <DB_User_name>
           [-p <DB_User_password>] [-q]

Where Spatial_Ref_Opts is
           [-x <xoffset,yoffset,xyscale>]
           [-z <zoffset,zscale>]
           [-m <moffset,mscale>]
           [-G {<projection_ID> |
           file=<proj_file_name>}]

sdelayer   -o alter -l <table,column>
           [-e <entity_mask>] [-M <minimum_id>]
           [-S <layer_description_str>]
           [-k <config_keyword>] [-i <service>]
           [-s <server_name>][-D <database>]
           [-g <new_grid_size>] [-E <{empty | calc
           | xmin,ymin,xmax,ymax}>]
           [-G {<projection_ID> |
           file=<proj_file_name>}]
           -u <DB_User_name>
           [-p <DB_User_password>] [-N] [-q]

sdelayer   -o {grant | revoke} -l  <table,column>
           -U <user>
           -A <SELECT,UPDATE,INSERT,DELETE>
           [-i <service>] [-s <server_name>]
           [-D <database>] -u <DB_User_name>
           [-p <DB_User_password>] [-I] [-q]

sdelayer   -o {describe | describe_long}
           [{-O <owner> | -l <table,column>}]
           [-i <service>] [-s <server_name>]
           [-D <database>] -u <DB_User_name>
           [-p <DB_User_password>] [-q]

sdelayer   -o list -l <table,column> -v <shape_id>
           [-i <service>] [-s <server_name>]
           [-D <database>]  -u <DB_User_name>
           [-p <DB_User_password>] [-q]

sdelayer   -o delete -l <table,column>
           [-i <service>] [-s <server_name>]
           [-D <database>] -u <DB_User_name>
           [-p <DB_User_password>] [-N] [-q]

sdelayer   -o truncate -l <table,column>
           [-i <service>] [-s <server_name>]
           [-D <database>] -u < DB_User_name>
           [-p <DB_User_password>] [-N] [-q]

sdelayer   -o {stats | si_stats}
           -l <table,column> [-i <service>]
           [-s <server_name>]
           [-D <database>] -u <DB_User_name>
           [-p <DB_User_password>] [-q]

sdelayer   -o {load_only_io | normal_io}
           -l <table,column> [-i <service>]
           [-s <server_name>] [-D <database>]
           -u <DB_User_name>
           [-p <DB_User_password>] [-q]

sdelayer   -o register [-e <entity_mask>]
           -l <table,column>
           [-k <config_keyword>]
           [-S <layer_description_str>]
           [-i <instance>] [-s <server_name>]
           -u <DB_User_name>
           [-p <DB_User_password>] [-q]

sdelayer   -h

sdelayer   -?
```

Operations

add	Adds a new map layer
alter	Modifies layer definition values
grant	Grants access to a layer for a user
revoke	Revokes access to a layer for a user
describe	Lists map layer definitions (short form). If a layer is not specified, lists all layers.
describe_long	Lists map layer definitions (long form). If a layer is not specified, lists all layers.
list	Lists the fields of a shape record including the point values for all points that define the shape of the feature
delete	Deletes an entire map layer. All shapes and the layer definition are permanently removed. The business table is not deleted.
truncate	Deletes all shape records in the map layer. The layer definition remains.
stats	Reports layer statistics
si_stats	Reports spatial index statistics
load_only_io	Sets the I/O mode of the layer to load-only, allowing only store and replace I/O operations. Use load-only mode when performing large inserts to avoid the continuous update of the layer indexes.

Operations (continued)

normal_io	Sets the I/O mode of the layer from load-only I/O mode to normal I/O mode
register	Registers a column defined with using Oracle Spatial Geometry Type, Oracle Spatial Normalized Type, Spatial DataBlade, or DB2 Spatial Extender

Options

-A	Type of access: SELECT, UPDATE, INSERT, or DELETE
-D	Database or data source name. Not supported by all RDBMSs.
-e	Entity types allowed (npslaAc3+M).

n	Nil
p	Point shapes
s	Line (spaghetti) shapes
l	Simple line (line string) shapes
a	Area shapes
A	Annotation
c	CAD data
3	Three-dimensional shapes can be added to the entity type mask only with the '-o add' operation
+	Multipart shapes
M	Measures on coordinates. The [-m] option is required if measures on coordinates are a defined shape type.
	Measures can be added to the entity type mask only with the "-o add" operation.

Adding a new entity type allows users to store shapes defined as the new entity type. Removing a previously allowed entity type will delete all shapes of the removed entity type.

-E	Layer envelope. There are three options:

Options (continued)

	empty	Sets the layer envelope to an empty envelope
	calc	Calculates the layer envelope
	xmin,ymin,xmax,ymax	
		Sets the envelope to the specified values
-f	(ArcSDE for Oracle only) Initial number of features and the average number of points per feature. These are used to calculate the initial and next extent of the layers's F and S tables. You cannot use this option with the -k option.	
-g	Map layer grid sizes. Grid cell sizes for levels 2 and 3 are optional. Examples are "-g 200" or "-g 200,1000,4000".	
-G	Coordinate system specifier. When used with the "alter" operation, it changes the layer's metadata, not the data itself. <projection_id>—coordinate system ID (see the pedef.h file for the integer codes). file=<proj_file_name>—file containing coordinate system description string.	
-h	Prints usage and options	
-i	ArcSDE service name	
-I	Inherit grant privilege. The "grant option" is included with the granted privilege. For example, if user A grants user B update privileges on a table, the -I option indicates that user A also wants to grant user B	

Options	(continued)
	the ability to grant other users update privileges on a particular table.
-k	Layer configuration keyword present in SDEHOME/etc/dbtune.sde. The storage parameters specific to the layer will be found under the specified keyword. You cannot use this option with the -f option.
-l	The business table and its spatial column. If you are not the owner of the table, you must qualify the table name as "owner.table".
-m	Measure offset and scale, separated by a comma
-M	Minimum feature ID. New shape IDs are assigned the larger of the minimum ID or the maximum assigned ID + one.
-N	No verification is performed—the operation begins immediately after being invoked
-o	Operation
-O	The owner of the layer
-p	ArcSDE user RDBMS password
-q	Quiet; all titles and warnings are suppressed
-R	Spatial reference ID (SRID)
-s	ArcSDE server hostname (default: localhost)
-S	Map layer description string (up to 63 characters)

Options	(continued)
-t	Allowed Storage type. Values are B (ArcSDE binary), N (normalized), W (well-known binary), or Q (SQL ADT)
-u	ArcSDE user RDBMS username
-U	ArcSDE user RDBMS username—the user to grant or revoke layer access to
-v	Shape ID
-x	The x and y offsets and scale values, separated by commas—the default is 0.0, 0.0, 1.0
-z	The z offset and scale values, separated by a comma
-?	Prints usage and options (use "-\?" on C shell)

Discussion

Before creating a new feature class (layer), make sure that enough space is available on your system.

Calculate the x-,y-, and z-scale values for the feature class (layer) by using the size of the service area and how much resolution is needed for the data. Coordinates are truncated if the scales are too small. For example, if the scale is set to 100 for coordinates in meters, then the unit of resolution is centimeters. Precision less than a centimeter is not stored. To set the unit of resolution to millimeters, increase the scale to 1,000. For more information on offsets and scales, see the previous sections.

Given this feature class specification:

```
RDBMS table name:        victoria
RDBMS column name:       parcels
Feature types:           multipart polygons
                         and annotation
Location:                victoria
Initial # of features:   10000
Avg points per feature:  10
Spatial index grid:      Level 1 - 1000 meters
xy offset:               0,0
xy scale:                200
z offset:                0
z scale:                 200
Coordinate system:       28355 (GDA1994 zone 55)
                         Geographic extent
```

The following command will create a feature class (layer):

```
$ sdelayer -o add -l victoria,parcels -e
aA3+ -g 1000,0,0 -x 0,0,200 -z 0,200 -G
28355 -f 10000,10 -u av -p mo -i esri_80
```

This command uses sdelayer to create a new layer with the above specifications. New empty layer tables are created.

The x,y offsets and scale are optional. If unspecified, they default to 0, 0, 1.

The register operation allows you to create a feature class (layer) from an RDBMS table that contains a column defined as a spatial data type. To date, ArcSDE supports four different implementations of RDBMS spatial data types: Oracle Spatial Geometry Type, Oracle Spatial Normalized Type, Spatial DataBlade, and DB2 Spatial Extender. Tables created with one of these spatial data types and populated using the RDBMS SQL interface or some other third party interface can be added to the ArcSDE database by registering the existing tables as ArcSDE feature classes (layers). The register command updates the ArcSDE data dictionary tables and, in the case of the ESRI Spatial DataBlade and the DB2 Data Extender, adds the SE_ROW_ID column to the table to facilitate ArcSDE logging.

```
$ sdelayer -o register -l victoria,parcels -
u av -p mo -i esri_80
```

The grant and revoke operations control access to feature classes (layers). The grant operation allows the owner of a feature class (layer) to provide either SELECT, INSERT, UPDATE, or DELETE privileges to other users or roles. The revoke operation allows the owner to rescind previously granted privileges.

The following two commands grant and then revoke select privileges from user "bob".

```
$ sdelayer -o grant -l victoria,parcels -U
bob -A SELECT -u av -p mo -i esri_80
$ sdelayer -o revoke -l victoria,parcels -U
bob -A SELECT -u av -p mo -i esri_80
```

You can list a feature class (layer) definition by using the ArcSDE feature class administration utility. All fields that define a feature class (layer) are displayed on the screen. To list all available feature classes (layer) for the current server, use:

```
$ sdelayer -o describe -u av -p mo -i
esri_40
```

The system responds with something like this:

```
ESRI SDE Layer Administration Utility Wed Feb  5
16:39:55 1997
```

```
------------------------------------------------
Table Owner          : AV
Table Name           : BORDERS
Spatial Column       : FID
Layer id             : 1
Entities             : a
Layer Type           : SDE
I/O Mode             : NORMAL
User Privileges      : SELECT, UPDATE
Layer Configuration  : DEFAULTS

------------------------------------------------
Table Owner          : AV
Table Name           : BOUNDARIES
Spatial Column       : BOUNDARY
Layer id             : 2
Entities             : a
Layer Type           : SDE
I/O Mode             : NORMAL
User Privileges      : SELECT, UPDATE, INSERT
Layer Configuration  : DEFAULTS

------------------------------------------------
```

```
------------------------------------------------
Table Owner          : AV
Table Name           : MINOR_ROADS
Spatial Column       : ROAD_LAYER
Layer id             : 3
Entities             : s
Layer Type           : SDE
I/O Mode             : NORMAL
User Privileges      : SELECT
Layer Configuration  : DEFAULTS

------------------------------------------------
```

To display the definition for a particular feature class (layer), specify the table and column name with the -l option.

```
$ sdelayer -o describe -l borders,fid -u av
-p mo -i esri_40
```

The system responds with something like this:

```
ESRI SDE Layer Administration Utility Wed Feb  5
16:28:14 1997
```

```
------------------------------------------------
Table Owner          : AV
Table Name           : BORDERS
Spatial Column       : FID
Layer id             : 1
Entities             : a
Layer Type           : SDE
I/O Mode             : NORMAL
User Privileges      : SELECT, UPDATE
Layer Configuration  : DEFAULTS

------------------------------------------------
```

You can list information about a feature's shape by using its shape ID. Get the shape ID by using sdetable's "list" operation.

Specifying a shape ID returns the shape fields and coordinates. Some shapes may have so many points that you can't view all the information as it's displayed. To control the display of the shape information, list the detailed feature information with a pagination program or redirect it to a file for later viewing or printing.

The following example displays a shape's detail and pipes the output through the "more" filter, allowing you to page through the information.

```
$ sdelayer -o list -l victoria,parcels -v
1012 -u av -p mo -i esri_40 | more
```

For feature classes (layers) that have been implemented using the binary schema (see 'Appendix C: ArcSDE table definitions'), deleting an ArcSDE feature class (layer) drops the RDBMS spatial tables (the F and S tables) and removes the definition of the feature class (layer) from the LAYERS and GEOMETRY_COLUMNS tables.

For feature classes (layers) implemented with the normalized schema (see 'Appendix C: ArcSDE table definitions'), the geometry table is dropped. The business table's spatial column is nulled and the feature class (layer) definition is removed from the LAYERS and GEOMETRY_COLUMNS table.

Under the spatial types and functions implementation, the spatial column is nulled and the feature class (layer) definition is removed from the LAYERS and GEOMETRY_COLUMNS table.

The business table still exists and is registered. To completely remove the business table, use "sdetable -o delete".

If a user has the feature class (layer) locked, sdelayer will return an error. You can use the sdemon "info" operation to make sure the feature class (layer) is not locked. The sdemon "kill" operation can remove the process that locked the feature class (layer). This is an abrupt solution and should only be used when

necessary. If circumstances permit, you should inform everyone that the feature class (layer) is going to be removed and provide application programmers with enough time to remove references to the feature class (layer) from their programs.

Use the sdelayer administration utility to delete the feature class (layer).

```
$ sdelayer -o delete -l victoria,parcels -u
av -p mo -i esri_80
```

The "truncate" operation removes the records from the feature class (layer) but does not drop the tables. However, the records of the business table are not removed. To remove these and the feature class (layer) tables, use sdetable with the "truncate" operation.

```
$ sdelayer -o truncate -l victoria,parcels
-u av -p mo -i esri_80 -N
```

Using the "alter" operation of sdelayer, you can modify the entity mask, spatial index grid cell sizes, coordinate system ID, description, envelope, or configuration keyword. The example below modifies the entity mask, configuration keyword, coordinate system ID, and description.

```
$ sdelayer -o alter -l victoria,parcels -e
al+ -k vict2 -G 4326 -S "Victoria Parcels"
-u av -p mo -i esri_40
```

This example changes the grid size.

```
$ sdelayer -o alter -l victoria,parcels -g
2000,0,0 -u av -p mo -i esri_40 -N
```

The "-N" option suppresses the prompt to verify the change in grid size.

The ArcSDE for Informix product implemented an rtree index as its spatial index. Changing the grid parameters with the "-g" option has no effect on an ArcSDE for Informix feature class (layer) since it does not have a grid index. The maintenance of the rtree index is automatic and cannot be adjusted.

You can change the grid sizes while the feature class (layer) is in normal or load-only I/O mode.

If the feature class (layer) is in normal I/O mode, the indexes on the spatial index table are dropped. While rebuilding the spatial index table, the feature class (layer) is set to load-only mode to disable read access. The indexes are rebuilt when the feature class (layer) is reset to normal I/O mode.

If the grid fields are updated while the feature class (layer) is in load-only I/O mode, the spatial index is rebuilt with the new grid sizes when you reset the feature class (layer) to normal I/O mode.

The sdelayer's envelope option has three keywords: "empty", "calc", and "xmin,ymin,xmax,ymax".

Setting it to "empty" will force an ArcSDE client to calculate the feature class's (layer's) envelope on the fly. This can be time-consuming.

When the feature class (layer) is in normal I/O mode, the envelope is automatically updated whenever a feature that extends the current envelope is added. The envelope is not updated while the feature class (layer) is in load-only I/O mode but is recalculated to the full extent when the feature class (layer) is reset to normal I/O mode.

Use "xmin,ymin,xmax,ymax" to set the envelope explicitly (for example, a study area). However, since the envelope is dynamically maintained, it will be extended to include new features that are added outside the extent set by "xmin,ymin,xmax,ymax".

The sdelayer command always creates a feature class (layer) in normal I/O mode. The load-only I/O mode is provided to make the bulk data loading processes more efficient. Load-only I/O mode allows shape storage and modification but disables retrieval.

To modify the I/O mode, use the "load_only_io" or "normal_io" operations.

```
$ sdelayer -o load_only_io -l
victoria,parcels -u av -p mo -i esri_40
```
or
```
$ sdelayer -o normal_io -l victoria,parcels
-u av -p mo -i esri_40
```

When the feature class (layer) administration utility returns a feature class (layer) to normal I/O mode, the spatial index table and database indexes are rebuilt. If the operation does not complete successfully for any reason, the feature class (layer) is left in load-only mode.

When a feature class (layer) is in load-only I/O mode, the unique index is removed from the feature class's (layer's) spatial column. When the index is absent, it's possible to enter nonunique values into the spatial column with a non-ArcSDE application. No applications besides ArcSDE should ever update the spatial column. Database administrators should be aware of the increased vulnerability of the spatial column when the feature class (layer) is in load-only I/O mode.

You can use sdelayer to display statistics about a feature class (layer) including feature entity type counts, total number of shapes, minimum and maximum shape number, the date of the last shape modification, the number of points in the largest shape, minimum and maximum linear shape lengths, minimum and maximum polygon areas, and the feature class (layer) envelope. The following command will display statistics for the parcels feature class (layer):

```
$ sdelayer -o stats -l victoria,parcels -u
av -p mo -i esri_40
```

The sdelayer command's spatial index statistics operation, "si_stats", can help you determine optimum spatial index grid sizes. Optimum grid cell sizes depend on the spatial size of all features, the variation in spatial feature size, and the types of searches to be performed on the feature class (layer).

Below is a sample output generated by "si_stats":

```
$ sdelayer -o si_stats -l victoria,parcels
-u av -p mo -i esri_40

SDE Layer Administration Utility Tue Oct 8
17:48:22 1996
_____

Layer 1 Spatial Index Statistics:
Level 1,   Grid Size 200 (Meters)
|_____
| Grid Records: 978341
| Shape Records: 627392
| Grids/Shape Ratio: 1.56
| Avg. Shapes per Grid: 18.26
| Max. Shapes per Grid: 166
| % of Shapes Wholly Inside 1 Grid: 59.71
|_____
|         Spatial Index Record Count By Group
|Grids:   <=4    >4  >10  >25  >50 >100 >250 >500
|_____  ___  _ __  _ __  _ __  __ __  _ __ __ __ __
|Shapes: 627392 0    0    0    0    0   0    0
|% Total:  100%  0%   0%   0%   0%   0%  0%   0%
|_____
|Level 2,   Grid Size 1600 (Meters)
|_____
| Grid Records: 70532
| Shape Records: 36434
| Grids/Shape Ratio: 1.94
| Avg. Shapes per Grid: 18.21
| Max. Shapes per Grid: 82|
| % of Shapes Wholly Inside 1 Grid: 45.35
|_____
|         Spatial Index Record Count By Group
|Grids:   <=4    >4  >10  >25  >50  >100  >250 500
|_____
|shapes: 35682 752 87   17   3    0    0    0
|%Total: 97%   2%  0%   0%   0%   0%   0%   0%
|_____
```

As the output shows, for each defined spatial index level in the feature class definition, the following values and statistics are printed:

- Grid level and cell size.

- Total spatial index records for the current grid level.

- Total shapes stored for the current grid level.

- Ratio of spatial index records per shape.

- Shape counts and percentages by group that indicate how shapes are grouped within the spatial index at this grid level. The column headings have the following meaning (where "N" is the number of grid cells):

<=N   Number of shapes and percentage of total shapes that fall within <= N grid cells

>N   Number of shapes and percentage of total shapes that fall within > N grid cells

Notice that the ">" groupings include count values from the next group. For instance, the ">4" group count represents the number of shapes that require more than four grid records as well as more than 10, and so on.

- Average number of shapes per grid.

- Maximum number of shapes per grid. This is the maximum number of shapes indexed into a single grid.

- Percentage of shapes wholly inside one grid. This is the percentage of all shapes wholly contained by one grid record.

The output sample shows spatial index statistics for a feature class that uses two grid levels: one that specifies a grid size of 200 meters, the other a grid size of 1,600 meters. When a shape requires more than four spatial index records, it is automatically promoted to the next grid level if one is defined. That is, in no case will a shape generate more than four grid records if more than one grid level exists. If a higher grid level doesn't exist, then a shape can have more than four grid records.

In the example above, 627,392 features are indexed through grid level 1. Because the system automatically promotes shapes that need more than four spatial index records to the next defined grid level, all 627,392 shapes for grid level 1 are indexed with four grid records or less. Grid level 2 is the last defined grid level, so shapes indexed at this level are allowed to be indexed with more than four grid records.

At grid level 2, there are a total of 36,434 shapes and 70,532 spatial index records: 35,682 shapes are indexed with four grid records or fewer, 752 shapes are indexed with more than four grid records, 87 shapes are indexed with more than 10, 17 shapes with more than 25, and three shapes with more than 50 grid records. Percentage values below each column show how the shapes are dispersed through the eight groups.

ArcSDE administration commands: sdelocator

This command manages ArcSDE locators.

Usage syntax

```
sdelocator    -o list [-T <{t|v|d}>]
              [-i <service>] [-s <server_name>]
              [-D <database>] -u <DB_User_name>
              [-p <DB_User_password>] [-q]

sdelocator    -o create -n <locator_name>
              -f <locator_properties_file>
              -T <{t|v}>
              [-S <locator_description>]
              [-i <service>] [-s <server_name>]
              [-D <database>] -u <DB_User_name>
              [-p <DB_User_password>] [-q]

sdelocator    -o delete {-n <locator_name> | -I
              <locator_id>} [-i <service>] [-s
              <server_name>] [-D <database>]
              -u <DB_User_name>
              [-p <DB_User_password>] [-q]

sdelocator    -o describe [-n <locator_name> | <-I
              locator>] [-i <service>]
              [-s <server_name>] [-D <database>]
              -u <DB_User_name>
              [-p <DB_User_password>] [-q]

sdelocator    -o refresh {-n <locator_name> | -I
              <locator_id>} [-i <service>]
              [ -s <server_name>] [-D <database>]
              -u <DB_User_name>
              [-p <DB_User_password>] [ -q]

sdelocator    -h
sdelocator    -?
```

Operations

list	List the locators for the service
create	Create a locator from the property file
delete	Delete the specified locator
describe	Describe the locator properties—if no locator is specified, all locators are described
refresh	Refresh locator indices

Options

-D	Database name
-f	Locator properties file
-h	Prints usage and options
-i	ArcSDE service name
-I	Locator ID
-n	Locator name
-o	Operation
-p	ArcSDE user RDBMS password
-q	Quiet
-s	ArcSDE server hostname (default: localhost)
-S	Locator description string
-T	Locator type (t: template, d: system defined, v: validated)
-u	ArcSDE user RDBMS username
-?	Prints usage and options (use "-\?" on C shell)

Discussion

The sdelocator command manages the ArcSDE metadata of a locator.

The "create" operation reads the locator's properties from a property file and, if the locator does not already exist in the SDE.LOCATORS table, adds an entry. The locator's properties are stored in the SDE.METADATA table.

The format of the locator property file must conform to the guidelines listed in *Modeling Our World*. The locator type option "-T" must specify the type of locator that will be created, either using a template or validated.

```
sdelocator -o create -n "US Streets" -f
C:\locators\us_strts.loc -T v -S US STREETS
-i esri_80 -u av -p mo
```

The "delete" operation removes a locator's metadata from the SDE.LOCATORS and SDE.METADATA table.

```
sdelocator -o delete -n "US Streets" -i
esri_80 -u av -p mo
```

The "list" operation provides a list of the locators in the ArcSDE server. The listing includes the locator ID, type, name, owner, category, and description.

```
sdelocator -o list  -i esri_80 -u av -p mo
```

```
ESRI SDE Attribute Administration Utility
Mon Oct 25 14:47:56 1999
```

ID	T	Name	Owner	Category	Description
141	t	SDE Feature Class	SDE	Address	SDE Feature Class
147	t	US Streets ESRI N'wide	SDE	Address	US Streets ESRI N'wide
148	v	Redlands	SERGEY	Address	SDE Feature Class
149	v	US Streets	SERGEY	Address	US Streets ESRI N'wide

The list operation can be qualified with the locator type option -T to list only those locators of a certain type.

```
sdelocator -o list -T t -i esri_80 -u av -p
mo
```

```
ESRI SDE Attribute Administration Utility Mon Oct
25 14:47:56 1999
```

ID	T	Name	Owner	Category	Description
141	t	SDE Feature Class	SDE	Address	SDE Feature Class
147	t	US Streets ESRI N'wide	SDE	Address	US Streets ESRI N'wide

The "describe" operation displays the properties of a locator.

```
sdelocator -o describe -n  "US Streets" -i
esri_80 -u av -p mo
```

```
;;;;;;;;;;;;;;;;;;;;;;;;;;;;;;;;;;;;;;;;;;;;;;;;;;;;;;;;;;;;;;;;;;;;;;;
; Description = "US Streets ESRI Nationwide"
; ID          = 139
; Type        = SE_LOCATOR_VALIDATED
; Owner       = SERGEY
;;;;;;;;;;;;;;;;;;;;;;;;;;;;;;;;;;;;;;;;;;;;;;;;;;;;;;;;;;;;;;;;;;;;;;;
Category = Address
CLSID                    = {04FCADCF-ED3B-11D2-9F48-00C04F8ED1C4}
UICLSID                  = {AE5A3A0E-F756-11D2-9F4F-00C04F8ED1C4}
Fields                   = Street
Fields                   = City
Fields                   = State
Fields                   = Zip
FieldNames.0             = Address
FieldNames.0             = Addr
FieldNames.1             = City
FieldNames.2             = State
FieldNames.2             = State_Abbr
FieldNames.3             = Zip
FieldNames.3             = Zipcode
FieldsRequired           = TRUE
FieldsRequired           = FALSE
FieldsRequired           = FALSE
FieldsRequired           = FALSE
FieldSizes               = 48
FieldSizes               = 16
FieldSizes               = 5
FieldSizes               = 2
Locator.Library          = libmtchloc
Locator.CLSID            = {D9052385-AB46-11d2-AADA-00C04FA379E3}
Locator.FactoryLibrary   = libmtchloc
Query.Library            = libmtchloc
Query.CLSID              = {C9A0D86C-C1D3-11d2-AAE4-00C04FA379E3}
MKeyField                = XX
MKeyField                = CT
MKeyField                = SA
MKeyField                = ZP
FileMAT                  = stmap.mat
FileSTN                  = stmap.stn
```

```
IntFileMAT                = stm_int.mat
IntFileSTN                = stm_int.stn
IntersectionConnectors    = &
MinimumMatchScore         = 60
MinimumCandidateScore     = 10
EndOffset                 = 0.9
SideOffset                = 0.00001
SpellingSensitivity       = 60
Ref.File                  =
\\metro\metro11\BMSource\streets\usa.edg
MKeyAlias.HN              = House Number
MKeyAlias.PD              = Prefix Direction
MKeyAlias.PT              = Prefix Type
MKeyAlias.SN              = Street Name
MKeyAlias.ST              = Suffix Type
MKeyAlias.SD              = Suffix Direction
MKeyAlias.ZN              = Zone
MKeyAlias.P1              = Prefix Direction 1
MKeyAlias.E1              = Prefix Street Type 1
MKeyAlias.S1              = Street Name 1
MKeyAlias.T1              = Suffix Street Type 1
MKeyAlias.D1              = Suffix Direction 1
MKeyAlias.P2              = Prefix Direction 2
MKeyAlias.E2              = Prefix Street Type 2
MKeyAlias.S2              = Street Name 2
MKeyAlias.T2              = Suffix Street Type 2
MKeyAlias.D2              = Suffix Direction 2
CandidateMode             = FALSE
SupportIntersections      = TRUE
Interpolate               = TRUE
InputAddressType          = 0
Mode                      = 0
WriteLatLongFields        = 0
WriteStandardizedAddressField = 0
```

ArcSDE administration commands: sdelog

This command administers log files.

Usage syntax

```
sdelog    -?

sdelog    -h

sdelog    -o alter -L <logfile> -k
          <PERSISTENT,TEMPORARY> [-O <Owner>]
          [-i <service>] [-s <server_name>]
          [-D <database>] -u <DB_User_name>
          [-p <DB_User_password>] [-N] [-q]

sdelog    -o clean [-O <Owner>] [-i <service>]
          [-s <server_name>]
          [-D <database>] -u <DB_User_name>
          [-p <DB_User_password>] [-N] [-A]
          [-q]

sdelog    -o delete -L <logfile> [-O <Owner>]
          [-i <service>] [-s <server_name>]
          [-D <database>] -u <DB_User_name>
          [-p <DB_User_password>] [-N] [-q]

sdelog    -o display -L <logfile> [-O <Owner>]
          [-i <service>] [-s <server_name>]
          [-D <database>] -u <DB_User_name>
          [-p <DB_User_password>] [-q]

sdelog    -o grant -U <user> [-O <owner>]
          [-i <service>] [-s {server_name>]
          [-D <database>] -u <DB_User_name>]
          [-p <DB_User_password>] [-q]

sdelog    -o list [{-O <Owner> | -l
          table,column> | -T <table>}]
          [-i <service>] [-s <server_name>]
          [-D <database>] -u <DB_User_name>
          [-p <DB_User_password>] [-q]

sdelog    -o revoke -U <user> [-O <owner>]
          [-i <service>] [-s {server_name>]
          [-D <database>] -u <DB_User_name>]
          [-p <DB_User_password>] [-q]
```

```
sdelog    -o truncate -l <logfile> [-O <Owner>]
          [-i <service>]
          [-s <server_name>] [-D <database>]
          -u <DB_User_name>
          [-p <DB_User_password>] [-N] [-q]
```

Operations

alter	Modify log file persistence
clean	Delete all temporary log files
delete	Delete a single log file
display	Print the contents of a log file
grant	Grant access to the owner's log files for a user
list	List a user's log files
revoke	Revoke access from the owner's log files for a user
truncate	Delete the contents of a log file

Options

-A	Deletes all log files: temporary, persistent, and old format log files
-D	Database name
-h	Prints usage and options
-i	ArcSDE service name
-k	Configuration keyword, either TEMPORARY or PERSISTENT
-l	Layer table and column names
-L	Log file name (not containing user)
-N	No verification is performed—the operation begins immediately after being invoked
-o	Operation
-O	Owner of the log file
-p	ArcSDE user RDBMS password
-q	Quiet; all titles and warnings are suppressed
-s	ArcSDE server hostname (default: localhost)
-T	Table name
-u	ArcSDE user RDBMS username
-U	ArcSDE user RDBMS username—the user who will be granted access to a log file or who will have access permissions to a log file revoked
-?	Prints usage and options (use "-\?" on C shell)

Discussion

Both the "delete" and "clean" operations of sdelog will remove log files. The "clean" operation by default removes a user's temporary log files.

```
$ sdelog -o clean -u av
```

Specify the "-N" option if you don't want to be prompted.

```
$ sdelog -o clean -u av -N
```

Specify the "-A" option to delete all of a user's log files: temporary, persistent, and pre-SDE 3 style.

```
$ sdelog -o clean -u av -N -A
```

The "delete" operation of the log file administration command removes a single log file. Again you may enter the "-N" option to suppress the verification prompt.

```
$ sdelog -o delete -L logBCAa06599 -u av -N
```

You can list the log files in a user's directory with the log file utility "list" operation. The list includes the name of the log file, the feature class internal ID, the current state of the log file, the number of shape records referenced, and the date and time the log file was last modified.

```
$ sdelog -o list -u av
```

ESRI SDE Logfile Administration Utility Wed Oct
14 14:08:21 1998

Name	Layer	State	Records	Time Last Modified

Name	Layer	State	Records	Time Last Modified
colog	9	UP	29	1998-10-14 12:42:30
citylog	5	SP	65	1998-10-14 12:42:32
ci_log	5	UT	11	1998-10-14 12:58:34
ci_log	5	ST	11	1998-10-14 12:58:34

The state column describes whether the log file is unsorted,
sorted, temporary, or persistent. The codes are:

UP—unsorted, persistent
SP—sorted, persistent
UT—unsorted, temporary
ST—sorted, temporary

The log file utility "display" operation provides a list of shape
IDs contained in the log file. The header of the output displays
the log filename and the feature class internal ID number. The
shape IDs are displayed in a column below the Feature ID (FID)
heading.

```
$ sdelog -o display -L ci_log -u av
```

ESRI SDE Logfile Administration Utility Wed Oct
14 14:20:44 1998

Printing the contents of logfile ci_log on
layer 5

FID
34
133
146
158
211
221
276
277
294
546
549

ArcSDE administration commands: sdemon

This command is used to monitor and manage the ArcSDE service. You can use sdemon to start up, pause, resume, and shut down all connection activity and display current configuration parameters and server task information. Individual server tasks can also be managed.

Security
Current execution privileges are granted to the root or the ArcSDE administrator for the start operation only. All other operations may be executed by any user who knows the password.

Usage syntax

```
sdemon    -o status [-i <service>]
          [-H <sde_directory>][-s <server_name>]
          [-q]
sdemon    -o start [-p <DB_Admin_password>]
          [-i <service>] [-H <sde_directory>]
          [-s <server_name>]
sdemon    -o shutdown [-p <DB_Admin_password>]
          [-i <service>] [-H <sde_directory>]
          [-s <server_name>] [-N]
sdemon    -o pause [-p <DB_Admin_password>]
          [-i <service>] [-H <sde_directory>]
          [-s <server_name>]
sdemon    -o resume [-p <DB_Admin_password>]
          [-i <service>] [-H <sde_directory>]
          [-s <server_name>]
sdemon    -o info -I <{users | config | stats |
          locks | vars}> [-i <service>]
          [-H <sde_directory>][-s <server_name>]
          [-q]
sdemon    -o kill [-p <DB_Admin_password>]
          -t <{ all | pid }> [-i <service>]
          [-H <sde_directory>] [-s <server_name>]
          [-N]
```

```
sdemon    -h
sdemon    -?
```

Operations

status	Reports the service status
start	Starts the ArcSDE service if it's not running. Only the ArcSDE administrator or root can use this operation.
shutdown	Shuts down the ArcSDE service immediately if no server tasks are running. If server tasks are running, you're prompted to remove the running tasks before the shutdown takes place. If you use the "-N" option when shutting down, all server tasks stop and the system shuts down immediately.
pause	Disallows further client connection requests to be processed. No client tasks are allowed to connect to ArcSDE servers through this ArcSDE service.
resume	Allows client connection requests to be processed again. Client tasks are allowed to connect to ArcSDE servers through this ArcSDE service.
info	Displays information about users, configuration, statistics, locks, or environment variables
kill	Kills all or a specified connection to the service

Options

-h	Prints usage and options
-H	ArcSDE home directory (SDEHOME)
-i	ArcSDE service name (not applicable for "start" option)
-I	Inquire about configuration, locks, statistics, users, or environment variables

	config	Displays current configuration variables
	locks	Displays lock information about processes that are holding locks
	stats	Displays process statistics for each ArcSDE client/server connection
	users	Lists users' connections to ArcSDE and associated process identifiers
	vars	Displays ArcSDE service environment variables

-N	No verification is performed—the operation begins immediately after being invoked
-o	Operation
-p	ArcSDE administrator RDBMS password
-q	Quiet; all titles and warnings are suppressed
-s	ArcSDE server hostname (default: localhost)
-t	Kills server tasks:

	all	Forcefully removes all server tasks
	pid	Removes the task identified by the process identifier

-?	Prints usage and options (use "-\?" in C shell)

ArcSDE administration commands: sderelease

This command can either list the ArcSDE server release or perform an upgrade on the server.

Usage syntax

```
sderelease -?

sderelease -h


sderelease -o upgrade [-p <DB_Admin_password>]
          [-N] [-q]
sderelease -o list  [-p <DB_Admin_password>]
          [-q]
```

Operations

upgrade	Upgrades the current ArcSDE version
list	Lists the installed ArcSDE version

Options

-h	Prints usage and options
-N	No verification—the operation begins immediately after being invoked
-o	Operation
-p	ArcSDE administrator RDBMS password
-q	Quiet; all titles and warnings are suppressed
-?	Prints usage and options (use "-\?" on C shell)

ArcSDE administration commands: sdeservice (Windows NT only)

This command manages the ArcSDE service on Windows NT.

Usage syntax

```
sdeservice -h

sdeservice -o create -p <DB_Admin_password>
            -l <license_server_name> [-q]
            [-H <sde_directory>]
            [-d <{ORACLE,SID |ORACLE8I,SID |
            SQLSERVER | DB2 | JET}>]
            [-i <service>] [-u <service_user>]
            [-P <service_user_password>]

sdeservice -o delete [-i <service>] [-a] [-q]

sdeservice -o register -r <{SDEHOME |
            SDE_DBA_PASSWORD | NLS_LANG}>
            -v <value> -p <DB_Admin_password>
            [-i <service>] [-q]

sdeservice -o unregister -r <{SDEHOME |
            SDE_DBA_PASSWORD | NLS_LANG}>
            -p <DB_Admin_password>[-i <service>]
            [- q]

sdeservice -o modify -r <{SDEHOME |
            SDE_DBA_PASSWORD |
            LICENSE_SERVER | NLS_LANG}>
            -p <old_DB_Admin_password>
            -v <new_value> [-i <service>] [-q]

sdeservice -o list [-i <service>] [-a] [-q]
```

Operations

create	Creates a service
delete	Deletes a service
register	Registers a service
unregister	Unregisters a service
modify	Modifies a service
list	Displays service information for all or a specified service

Options

-a	For the delete operation, delete all services. For the list operation, list the information of all services.
-d	An RDBMS whose service should start before ArcSDE. Optional if the RDBMS is on a remote machine. This must be in uppercase.
-h	Prints usage and options
-H	ArcSDE home directory (SDEHOME). Only needed if the SDEHOME variable isn't set or multiple services are in use.
-i	ArcSDE service name—only required if the service is not called "esri_sde"
-l	License server host computer name
-N	No verification is performed—the operation begins immediately after being invoked
-o	Operation
-p	ArcSDE administrator RDBMS password
-P	ArcSDE service user password (Windows NT login password)
-q	Quiet; all titles and warnings are suppressed
-r	Windows NT registry keyword

Options	(continued)
-u	ArcSDE service account user—must be a Windows NT user who has "administrator" permissions on the server computer. Include the domain name if needed. For example, if you're logged into the "AVWORLD" domain and your username is 'joe', enter "AVWORLD\joe". You should be logged in as this user when you create the service.
-v	Registry value
-?	Prints usage and options (use "-\?" on C shell)

Discussion

The sdeservice administration utility manages the ArcSDE services and registry entries on Windows NT platforms. Installing the ArcSDE software adds one service and several related registry entries, which include SDE_DBA_PASSWORD, SDEHOME, LICENSE_SERVER, and NLS_LANG.

The "create" and "delete" operations will add or delete the ArcSDE service entry, respectively . You can modify the registry values of SDEHOME, SDE_DBA_PASSWORD, LICENSE_SERVER, or NLS_LANG with the modify operation. You can also remove or re-create the SDEHOME or SDE_DBA_PASSWORD entries with the "unregister" and "register" operations. Normally, you'll only need to use the register operation after using unregister.

ArcSDE administration commands: sdetable

This command administers business tables and their data.

Usage syntax

```
sdetable    -o create -t <table> -d
            <column_definition>
            [-k <config_keyword>] [-i <service>]
            [-s <server_name>] [-D <database>]
            -u <DB_User_name>
            [-p <DB_User_password>] [-q]

sdetable    -o delete -t <table>
            [-i <service>] [-s <server_name>]
            [-D <database>]-u <DB_User_name>
            [-p <DB_User_password>] [-N] [-q]

sdetable    -o truncate -t <table>
            [-i <service>] [-s <server_name>]
            [-D <database>] -u <DB_User_name>
            [-p <DB_User_password>] [-N] [-q]

sdetable    -o list -t <table> -c <column> -v
            <column_value> [-i <service>]
            [-s <server_name>] [-D <database>]
            -u <DB_User_name>
            [-p <DB_User_password>] [-N] [-q]

sdetable    -o describe -t <table>
            [-i <service>] [-s <server_name>]
            [-D <database>] [-u <DB_User_name>] [-p
            <DB_User_password>] [-q]

sdetable    -o create_index -t <table>
            -n  <index> -c <column>
            [-k <config_keyword>] [-Q]
            [-i <service>] [-s <server_name>]
            [-D <database>] -u <DB_User_name>
            [-p <DB_User_password>] [-q]

sdetable    -o delete_index -n <index>
            [-t <table>] [-i <service>]
            [-s <server_name>] [-D <database>]
            -u <DB_User_name>
            [-p DB_User_password>] [-N] [-q]

sdetable    -o rename -t <table> -T <new_name>
            [-i <service>] [-s <server_name>]
            [-D <database>] -u <DB_User_name>
            [-p <DB_User_password>] [-N] [-q]

sdetable    -o {grant|revoke} -t <table>
            -U <user>
            -A <SELECT,UPDATE,INSERT,DELETE>
            [-i <service>] [-s <server_name>]
            [-D <database>] -u <DB_User_name>
            [-p <DB_User_password>] [-I] [-q]

sdetable    -o register -t <table>
            [{-c <row_id_column>
            -C {SDE | USER} } | {-C NONE}]
            [-L {off | on}] [-M <minimum_id>]
            [-S <table_description>]
            [-V <{single | multi}>]
            [-k <config_keyword>]
            [-H <{visible | hidden}>]
            [-i <service>] [-s <server_name>]
            [-D <database>] u <DB_User_name>
            [-p <DB_User_password>] [-q]

sdetable    -o unregister -t <table>
            [-i <service>] [-s <server_name>]
            [-D <database>]
            -u <DB_User_name>
            [-p <DB_User_password>] [-N] [-q]

sdetable    -o alter_reg -t <table>
            [{-c <row_id_column>
            -C {SDE | USER} } | {-C NONE}]
            [-L {off | on}] [-M <minimum_id>]
            [-S <table_description>]
            [-V <{single | multi}>]
            [-k config_keyword]
            [-H <{visible | hidden}>]
            [-i <service>] [-s <server_name>]
            [-D <database>]  -u <DB_User_name>
            [-p <DB_User_password>] [-N] [-q]
```

```
sdetable   -o describe_reg [{-U <user> | -t
           <table>}] [-i <service>]
           [-s <server_name>] [-D <database>]
           -u <DB_User_name>
           [-p DB_User_password>] [-q]

sdetable   -o create_view -T <view_name> -t
           <table1,table2,...tablen>
           -c <table_col1,table_col2..table_coln>
           [-a <view_col1,view_col2,...view_coln>]
           [-w <where_clause>] [-i <service>]
           [-s <server_name>] [-D <database>]
           -u <DB_User_name>
           [-p <DB_User_password>] [-N] [-q]

sdetable   -o create_im_view -T <view_name> -t
           <table_name> [-i <service>]
           [-s <server_name>] [-D <database>]
           -u <DB_User_name>
           [-p <DB_User_password>] [-N] [-q]

sdetable   -o delete_im_view -t <table_name>
           [-i <service>] [-s <server_name>]
           [-D <database>] -u <DB_User_name>
           [-p <DB_User_password>] [-N] [-q]

sdetable   -o update_dbms_stats -t <table_name>
           [ -K <keyword>]
           -m <{estimate | compute}>
           [-n <{ALL | <index_name>}>]
           [-i <service>]
           [-s <server_name>][-D <database>]
           [-u <DB_User_name>]
           [-p <DB_User_password>] [-N] [-q]

sdetable   -h

sdetable   -?
```

Operations

alter_reg	Modifies a registration entry
create	Creates a new table
create_im_view	Creates an intelligent multiversioned view
create_index	Creates an index on a table
create_view	Creates an RDBMS view
delete	Deletes a table—can be used to completely delete a layer
delete_im_view	Deletes an intelligent multiversioned view
delete_index	Deletes an index on a table
describe	Displays a table definition
describe_reg	Displays table registration entries
grant	Grants access to a table for a user
list	Lists column data for a given field value
register	Registers a table in the ArcSDE table registry
rename	Renames a table
revoke	Removes access to a table for a user
truncate	Deletes all records from a table
unregister	Removes a table from the ArcSDE table registry
update_dbms_stats	
	Updates RDBMS table and/or index statistics

Options

-a	A comma-separated list of a view column names—use if you want a view to have different column names
-A	Type of access: SELECT, UPDATE, INSERT, or DELETE
-c	Row ID column name. This option requires using "-C SDE" or "-C USER". If using the create_view operation, use a comma-separated list of column names.
-C	Row ID column type: SDE—SDE-maintained row_id column. USER—User-maintained row_id column. NONE—No row_id column. You can't use the "–c" option with this choice.
-d	Column definition
-D	Database or data source name. Not supported by all RDBMSs.
-h	Prints usage and options
-H	Registers the table as either visible or hidden
-i	ArcSDE service name
-I	Inherit grant privilege. The "grant option" is included with the granted privilege. For example, if user A grants user B update privileges on a table, the -I option indicates that user A also wants to grant user B the ability to grant other users update privileges on a particular table.
-k	Layer configuration keyword

Options (continued)

-K	Schema object keyword: a—A<registration_ID> table ("adds") b—<business table> d—D<Registration_ID> table ("deletes") f—F<Layer_id> table ("feature")
-L	Enable (on) or disable (off) a ROW_LOCK on a registered table
-m	Update RDBMS statistics mode—Oracle **only**
-M	Minimum row ID
-n	Index name
-N	No verification is performed—the operation begins immediately after being invoked
-o	Operation
-p	ArcSDE user RDBMS password
-q	Quiet; all titles and warnings are suppressed.
-Q	Index is unique
-s	ArcSDE server hostname (default: localhost)
-S	Registration entry description string
-t	Table name. If you do not own the table, qualify the table name as "owner.table". If using the create_view operation, use a comma-separated list of table names.
-T	New table name

Options	(continued)
-u	ArcSDE user RDBMS username
-U	ArcSDE user RDBMS username—the user to grant or revoke table access to OR who owns a table
-v	Column value
-V	Specify if the table is single or multiversioned
-w	SQL where clause
-?	Prints usage and options (use "-\?" on C shell)

Discussion

To create a business table, supply the table name and field specifications. The field specification uses standard SQL syntax to specify a field list, so you cannot use any SQL reserved words as field names. The field specification may use any data type defined by ANSI SQL89. The field specification of sdetable accepts ArcSDE standard data types, which it maps to RDBMS native data types. The standard ArcSDE data types are:

smallint(n)	where: $0 < n <= 4$
integer(n)	where: $4 < n <= 9$
float(n,m)	where: $0 < n <= 6, 0 < m <=$ RDBMS limit
double(n,m)	where: $6 < n <=$ RDBMS limit, $0 < m <$ RDBMS limit
string(n)	where: $0 < n <=$ RDBMS limit
blob	
date	

This command creates an attribute table:

```
$ sdetable -o create -t victoria -d "name
string(20), tot_pop integer(9)" -k vict -u
av -p mo -s ultra -i esri_80
```

The resulting table contains two columns: a string column called "name" and an integer column called "tot_pop".

The rename operation can be used to change the name of a table. Not all RDBMSs support table renaming.

```
$ sdetable  -o rename -t world -T world2000
-u av -p mo
```

To delete a business table, use the sdetable "delete" operation. The associated feature class (layer), if one exists, is deleted as well.

```
$ sdetable -o delete -t victoria -u av -p mo
-s ultra -i esri_40
```

Truncating deletes all the records of the business table and the associated feature class (layer), leaving the definition of the table and feature class (layer) intact.

```
$ sdetable -o truncate -t victoria -u av -p
mo -s ultra -i esri_40
```

To change a business table's specification, use the ALTER statement from the RDBMS's SQL utility.

To list the business table definition, use the "describe" operation. It lists the column name and the related data type and length in bytes for each column in the business table.

```
$ sdetable -o describe -t victoria -u av -p
mo -i esri_40
```

To list rows of a business table, you must specify the table, a column name, and a value of the specified column. An implicit query is performed on the table to fetch and display the rows that have a column equal to the value.

The command below lists the rows of the business table whose parcels column value equals 10:

```
$ sdetable -o list -t victoria -c parcels -v
10 -u av p mo -i esri_40
```

The "create_index" operation creates an index on a business table column. This example creates an index on column "parcel_no".

```
$ sdetable -o create_index -t victoria -c
parcel_no -n index1 -u av -p mo -i esri_40
```

You can create aggregate indexes by specifying a comma-separated list of columns. The example creates an aggregate index on the parcel_no and zone_no columns.

```
$ sdetable -o create_index -t victoria -c
parcel_no,zone_no -n index2 -u av -p mo
```

To remove an index from an attribute table, specify the index name.

The following command deletes the index "index1" from the business table:

```
$ sdetable -o delete_index -n index1 -u av
-p mo
```

Not all RDBMSs maintain unique index names, in which case you must qualify the index name with the table name (for example, victoria.index1).

You can also use sdetable to manage registered tables. To register a feature class (layer) called "world":

```
$ sdetable -o register -t world -u av -p mo
```

The above example allows most of the registration parameters to default. You can specify a particular column to use for the unique row ID column with "-c". If you do this, you also need to use "-C" to specify whether the row ID column is ArcSDE or user managed. To describe the newly registered table:

```
$ sdetable -o describe_reg -t world -u av -p
mo
```

```
ESRI SDE Attribute Administration Utility Tue Oct
20 17:00:36 1998
_____

Table Owner         : AV
Table Name          : WORLD
Registration Id     : 109
Dependent Objects   : Layer
Registration Date   : Thu Sep 17 11:32:19 1998
Config. Keyword     : DEFAULTS
User Privileges     : SELECT, UPDATE, INSERT,
                      DELETE
```

You can unregister or alter the registration entry of a table with the "unregister" and "alter_reg" operations, respectively.

The "alter_reg" operation is used to turn row locking on, reset the minimum ID to 1,000 , and change the table to hidden. Hidden tables do not appear in lists unless they are specified specifically.

```
$ sdetable -o alter_reg -t world -L on -M
1000 -H hidden -u av -p mo
```

The world feature class (layer) is unregistered with the unregister operation. As a result the logging can no longer be performed, and if the table was registered as multiversioned, all versions of the feature class are lost.

Views can be created with the "create_view" option. The views created are stored in your RDBMS just like any other view you would create with an SQL editor. You may create views that join several tables together up to the limit imposed by your RDBMS. However, just as ArcSDE imposes the limit of one spatial column per table, that limit also applies to views created by the "create_view" operation.

```
$ sdetable  -o create_view -T world_view -t
            "world,countries"  -c
            "world.population,
             world.gnp, countries.name,
            countries.feature"  -a
            "population,
            gross_national_product, name,
            feature" -w  world.cname =
            countries.name -u av -p mo
```

Intelligent multiversioned views are created with the "create_im_view" operation. These views provide direct SQL access to a multiversioned business table.

```
$ sdetable  -o create_im_view -T
world_imv_view -t world -u av -p mo
```

The delete_im_view operation drops a multiversioned view.

```
$ sdetable  -o delete_im_view -t world -u av
-p mo
```

The "update_dbms_stats" operation can be used to update the RDBMS statistics of a business table, the index of a business table, or all the indexes of a business table. All RDBMSs supported by ArcSDE maintain statistics about the business tables and indexes. Following a lot of changes to a table or index, the statistics for that data object become stale. As a rule of thumb, if more than 20 percent of the table has changed, you should use the "update_dbms_stats" operation on that table.

The statistics of all a table's indexes are automatically updated whenever you update the statistics of the table.

The mode option is specific to the RDBMS. For more information see the *ArcSDE Configuration and Tuning Guide for <RDBMS>* PDF file.

To update the statistics of a table and all its indexes, do not specify the "-n" option.

```
$ sdetable  -o update_dbms_stats -t world -m
compute -u av -p mo
```

To update the statistics of all the indexes but not the table and its indexes, specify the "-n all" option.

```
$ sdetable  -o update_dbms_stats -t world -m
estimate -n world_ix -u av -p mo
```

To update the statistics of an individual index, specify the -n option with the name of an index.

```
$ sdetable -o update_dbms_stats -t world -m
estimate -n all -u av -p mo
```

The "-K" option allows you to specify which ArcSDE schema object to analyze. One or any combination of the keyword values may be used. For example:

```
$ sdetable -o update_dbms_stats -k ad -m
estimate  -u av -p mo
```

This command updates the RDBMS statistics for the A<Registration_id> ("adds") and the D<Registration_ID> ("deletes") tables.

If no keyword value is given, the statistics for the business table and associated support tables will be updated.

ArcSDE administration commands: sde2cov

This command converts ArcSDE feature classes to ArcInfo coverages.

Usage syntax

```
sde2cov    -h

sde2cov    [-o create] -l <table,column> [-V
           <version_name>]
           -f <coverage,feature_class>
           [-P <{double | single}>] [-a <{none |
           all | file=<file_name>}>]
           [-w <"where_clause">] [-i <service>]
           [-s <server_name>] [-D <database>]
           -u <DB_User_name>
           [-p DB_User_password>]

sde2cov    [-o create] -L <log_file> [-V
           <version_name>]
           -f <coverage,feature_class>
           [-P <{double | single}>] [-a <{none |
           all | file=<file_name>}>]
           [-w <"where_clause">] [-i <service>]
           [-s <server_name>]
           [-D <database>] -u <DB_User_name>
           [-p <DB_User_password>]
```

Operations

create	Creates a new feature class in a coverage. An error is returned if the feature class exists (default).

Options

-a	Attribute mode:	
	none	Do not load any attributes
	all	Load all attribute columns (default)
	file=<file_name> File containing lines of the form <SDE_column> [INFO_item] The first part selects the SDE column; the second part (optional) allows a new item name to be specified.	
-D	Database name	
-f	Output feature class name of coverage, Map LIBRARIAN, or ArcStorm layer	
-h	Prints usage and options	
-i	ArcSDE service name	
-l	Input feature class table and spatial column name	
-L	The name of the log file to extract from	
-o	Operation	
-p	ArcSDE user RDBMS password	
-P	ArcInfo coverage's precision (default: double)	
-s	ArcSDE server hostname (default: localhost)	
-u	ArcSDE user RDBMS username	
-V	Version name. If specified, export only the data that belongs to the version.	
-w	SQL where clause	
-?	Prints usage and options (use "-\?" on C shell)	

Discussion

You must update the topology of any coverage produced by sde2cov. Run "CLEAN" on polygon and region coverages and "BUILD" or "CLEAN" on other feature classes (layers). You must then run "CREATELABELS" on the output coverage to assign label points to each polygon. You can export annotation to new subclasses of existing coverages. You can't export annotation into an existing subclass of an existing coverage. All other feature types must be exported to new coverages.

As the ArcSDE "multipart area" feature class (layer) equates to an ArcInfo coverage "region" feature, you must preserve the regions (and associated attribute data) in the resulting output coverage. Further reduction to composite polygon features could result in data loss and corruption.

Multipart lines with measures exported into route subclasses will produce coverages with an arc and a section at each vertex. You can reduce the number of arcs if the coverage is cleaned for lines using the "CLEAN" command. All section tables will remain after the "CLEAN" operation.

ArcSDE entity type to feature class mapping

ArcSDE entity type	Coverage feature class
point (p)	point, node
simple line, line (sl)	line
area (a)	polygon
multipart area (a+)	region.<subclass>
multipart lines with measures (slM+)	route.<subclass>
point, line, simple line, ANNO (pslA)	anno.<subclass>

Examples

1. Exporting multipart polygons to a region coverage:

```
$ sde2cov -o create -l world.cntry94,feature
-f country,region.cntry -P single -a all -u
world -p world
ESRI SDE: Layer to Coverage Loading Utility Fri
Sep  5 10:58:33 1997
```
_____

```
Exported 165 features from 'world.cntry94' into
country
SDE2Cov completed.
```

2. Exporting a subset of features with a where clause:

```
$ sde2cov -o create -l world.cities,feature
-f big,point -w 'population > 10000000' -a
all -u world -p world
ESRI SDE: Layer to Coverage Loading Utility Fri
Sep  5 11:02:15 1997
```
_____

```
Exported 11 features from 'world.cities' into big
SDE2Cov completed.
```

3. Exporting polygons from a multiversioned feature class (layer).

```
$ sde2cov -o create -l
world.countries,feature -f country,polygon
-V version10 -P single -a all -u world -p
world
ESRI SDE: Layer to Coverage Loading Utility Wed
Sep  15 11:38:13 1999
```
_____

```
Exported 273 features from 'world.countries' into
country
SDE2Cov completed.
```

ArcSDE administration commands: sde2shp

This command extracts features from an ArcSDE feature class (layer) or log file and writes them out to an ESRI shapefile.

Usage syntax

```
sde2shp   -h
```

From a feature class:

```
sde2shp   -o append -l <table,column>
          [-V <version_name>]
          -f <shape_file> -t <file_type>
          [-a <{all | file=<file_name>}>]
          [-w <"where_clause">] [-i <service>]
          [-s <server_name>]
          [-D <database>] -u <DB_User_name>
          [-p <DB_User_password>]

sde2shp   -o init -l <table,column>
          [-V <version_name>]
          -f <shape_file> -t <file_type>
          [-a <{all | file=<file_name>}>]
          [-w <"where_clause">] [-i <service>]
          [-s <server_name>]
          [-D <database>] -u <DB_User_name>
          [-p <DB_User_password>]
```

From a log file:

```
sde2shp   -o append -L <log_file>
          [-V <version_name>]
          -f <shape_file> -t <file_type>
          [-a <{all | file=<file_name>}>]
          [-w <"where_clause">] [-i <service>]
          [-s <server_name>] [-D <database>]
          -u <DB_User_name>
          [-p <DB_User_password>]
```

```
sde2shp   -o init -L <log_file>
          [-V <version_name>]
          -f <shape_file> -t <file_type>
          [-a <{all | file=<file_name>}>]
          [-w <"where_clause">] [-i <service>]
          [-s <server_name>][-D <database>]
          -u <DB_User_name>
          [-p <DB_User_password>]
```

Conversion table

ArcSDE feature	Output shape
point	point (If the output shapefile is a multipoint type, then each point feature is written out as a multipoint shape with one point.)
lines	arc
simple lines	arc
area	polygon
multipart	multipart (region)

Operations

append	Adds the features to existing features in the shapefile—creates the file if it doesn't already exist
init	Deletes the shapefile if it exists and then creates a new one

Options

-a	Attribute modes:

	all	Loads all attribute columns. If an attribute table exists, the incoming schema must be union compatible with the shapefile's dBASE table if using the append operation.

file=<file_name>
File containing lines of the form
<sde_column>[shape_column] [type] [width] [nDec].
The sde_column selects the column to output. The remaining optional items determine the new attribute column definitions. You can export feature table columns such as spatial_column.FID and spatial_column.AREA.

-D	Database or data source name. Not supported by all RDBMSs.
-f	Path to and name of the shapefile to create or add to
-h	Prints usage and options
-i	ArcSDE service name
-l	The map layer table and spatial column to extract from. These must exist, and the executing user must have read access. If you are not the owner of the table, you must qualify the table name as "owner.table".
-L	Name of the log file to extract from

Options	(continued)
-o	Operation
-p	ArcSDE user RDBMS password
-s	ArcSDE server hostname (default: localhost)
-t	Shapefile types (names are not case sensitive)

	point	Accepts only point features
	pointZ	Accepts points, z-values, and, optionally, measure values
	pointM	Accepts points and measures
	arc	Accepts line, simple line, and area features. Area features with donuts are accepted as multipart shapefile arc features.
	arcZ	Accepts linear features, z-values, and optionally, measure values
	arcM	Accepts linear features and measures.
	polygon	Accepts area features.
	polygonZ	Accepts area features, z-values, and, optionally, measure values
	polygonM	Accepts area features and measures
	multipoint	Accepts points and multipart points
	multipointZ	Accepts points, multipoints, z-values, and, optionally, measure values
	multipointM	Accepts points, multipoints, and measure values

-u	ArcSDE user RDBMS username

Options	(continued)
-V	Version name. If specified, export only the data that belongs to the version.
-w	SQL where clause to limit the features retrieved from the business table or log file
-?	Prints usage and options (use "-\?" on C shell)

ArcSDE administration commands: sde2tbl

This command converts an ArcSDE table format to an ArcSDE, dBASE, or INFO table.

Usage syntax

```
sde2tbl    -h

sde2tbl    -o append -t <table> -f <file_name>
           -T {dBASE | INFO | SDE} [-I]
           [-a <{all | file=<file_name>}>]
           [-c <commit_interval>]
           [-i <service>] [-s <server_name>]
           [-D <database>]-u <DB_User_name>
           [-p <DB_User_password>] [-v]
           [-w <"where_clause">]

sde2tbl    -o init -t <table> -f <file_name>
           -T {dBASE | INFO | SDE} [-I]
           [-a <{all | file=<file_name>}>]
           [-c <commit_interval>]
           [-i <service>] [-s <server_name>]
           [-D <database>] -u <DB_User_name>
           [-p <DB_User_password>] [-v]
           [-w <"where_clause">]

sde2tbl    -o create -t <table> -f <file_name> -T
           {dBASE | INFO | SDE} [-I]
           [-a <{all | file=<file_name>}>]
           [-c <commit_interval>]
           [-k <config_keyword>]
           [-w <"where_clause">]
           [-i <service>] [-s <server_name>]
           [-D <database>] -u <DB_User_name>
           [-p <DB_User_password>] [-v]
```

Operations

append	Adds records to an existing ArcSDE, dBASE, or INFO table (the default)
init	Deletes all records in an existing RDBMS table before importing new records
create	Creates a new table and imports records into it—an error is returned if the table already exists

Options

-a	Attribute modes:
	all Loads all columns (the default). If the table exists, the incoming schema must be union compatible with the table if using the append or init option.
	file=<file_name> File containing lines of the form <fr_colName> [to_colName] [type] [size] [nDecs] [NOT_NULL]
	The <fr_colName> selects the column to export, while the <to_colName> specifies the new column to load to. The allowed type, size, and nDecs (number of decimal places) values will vary according to each RDBMS.
-c	Commit rate (default is the AUTOCOMMIT value from giomgr.defs). Only used when the output table type is "SDE".
-D	Database or data source name—not supported by all RDBMSs
-f	Output table name—define the table type with the "-T" option.
-h	Prints usage and options
-i	ArcSDE service name
-I	Disable buffered inserts (default: ON). Only used when the output table type is SDE.

Options   (continued)

-k	Configuration keyword from dbtune.sde (default: DEFAULTS). Only used when the output table type is SDE.
-o	Operation
-p	ArcSDE user RDBMS password
-s	ArcSDE server hostname (default: localhost)
-t	Input ArcSDE table name
-T	Output table type, either dBASE, INFO, or SDE
-u	ArcSDE user RDBMS username
-v	Verbose option—reports records committed at the commit interval
-w	SQL where clause
-?	Prints usage and options (use "-\?" in C shell)

Discussion

The sde2tbl command converts ArcSDE tables into INFO and dBASE tables. You can also use sde2tbl to selectively copy columns from an ArcSDE table into a new ArcSDE table. The example below converts an ArcSDE table called block_attr into a dBASE table called census_data.

```
$ sde2tbl -o create -t block_attr -f
census_data -T dBASE -a all -u av -p mo
```

If the table already exists, you can add more records with the "append" operation. You can also remove the records from an existing table with the "init" operation before loading more records.

ArcSDE administration commands: sdeversion

This command allows the ArcSDE administrator to manage versions.

Usage syntax

```
sdeversion -o alter -V <version_name>
            [-d <description>]
            [-A <{public | protected | private}>]
            [-N] -u <DB_User_name>
            [-p <DB_User_password>]
            [-i <service>]  [-s <server_name>]
            [-D <database>] [-q]
sdeversion -o create -V <version_name>
            -P <parent_version>
            [-U]  [-A <{public | protected |
            private}>] [-d <description>]
            -u <DB_User_name>
            [-p <DB_User_password>]
            [-i <service>]
            [-s <server_name>][-D <database>][-q]
sdeversion -o delete -V <version_name> [-N]
            -u <DB_User_name>
            [-p <DB_User_password>]
            [-i <service>] [-s <server_name>]
            [-D <database>] [-q]
sdeversion -o rename -V <old_version_name>
            -n <new_version_name> [-N]
            -u <DB_User_name>
            [-p <DB_User_password>]
            [-i <service>] [-s <server_name>]
            [-D <database>] [-q]
sdeversion -o describe [-V <version_name>]
            [-w <"where_clause">]
            -u <DB_User_name>
            [-p <DB_User_password>]
            [-i <service>][-s <server_name>]
            [-D <database>] [-q]
```

```
sdeversion  -?
sdeversion  -h
```

Operations

alter	Modifies a version's definition
create	Creates a new version
delete	Deletes an existing version
rename	Renames an existing version
describe	Shows version descriptions

Options

-A	Access. Public, protected, or private
-d	Version description
-h	Prints usage and options
-i	ArcSDE service name
-n	New version name
.-N	No verification is performed—the operation begins immediately after being invoked
-o	Operation
-p	ArcSDE user RDBMS password
-P	Parent version name
-q	Quiet; all titles and warnings are suppressed
-s	ArcSDE server hostname (default: localhost)
-U	Generate unique version name by adding a suffix if necessary
-u	ArcSDE user RDBMS username
-V	Version name
-w	SQL where clause
-?	Prints usage and options (use "-\?" on C shell)

Discussion

The sdeversion command manages versions of a geodatabase. For more information on this topic, see *Building a Geodatabase*.

The "describe" option lists the current definition of an existing version.

```
$ sdeversion -o describe -V SDE.DEFAULT -u
sde -p sde
```

ESRI ArcSDE Version Administration Utility Thu Oct 28 06:21:24 1999

```
--------------------------------
Instance default version.
--------------------------------

Version Name:          SDE.DEFAULT
Version ID:            1
Parent Version Name:
Parent Version ID:     0
State ID:              3422
Access:                Public
Creation Time:         09/01/99 11:16:28
```

In the following example, we will create a new private version called "MY_VERSION", based on version "SDE.DEFAULT". As this will be a private version, only the person who creates it will have access to it.

```
$ sdeversion -o create -V MY_VERSION -P
SDE.DEFAULT -A private -d "Overpass
Design- Phase II" -u sde -p sde
```

The "-d" option allows you to add some descriptive text when creating the new version. This provides useful documentation as to the reasons for creating the new version.

The "alter" option allows you to alter the definition of a version. For example, you may wish to make the new version available to some coworkers but with read-only access permissions.

```
$ sdeversion -o alter -V MY_VERSION -A
protected -u sde -p sde
```

Only the version owner can alter, rename, or delete a version. You cannot delete "parent" versions until any dependent "child" versions have first been removed.

ArcSDE administration commands: sdexinfo

This command describes an ArcSDE export file.

Usage syntax

```
sdexinfo  -h
sdexinfo  [-o describe] -f <{export_file | -}>
sdexinfo  -o stats -f <{export_file | -}>
sdexinfo  -o list -f <{export_file | -}> [-s]
          [-a]
```

Operations

describe	Lists the export file header and attribute column definitions (the default)
stats	Performs the describe operation and lists statistical information
list	Performs the stats operation and lists partial or complete feature and attribute data values

Options

-a	Lists the attribute data values
-f	ArcSDE export filename. If "–", read from standard input
-h	Prints usage and options
-o	Operation
-s	Displays a detailed shape feature definition. Displays all fields of the feature definition including the point values.
-?	Prints usage and options (use "-\?" on C shell)

ArcSDE administration commands: shpinfo

This command reports information about a shapefile while preparing to load it into an ArcSDE feature class (layer).

Usage syntax

```
shpinfo    -h
shpinfo    [-o describe] -f <shape_file>
           [-d <{shape | sde | both}>]
shpinfo    -o stats -f <shape_file>
           [-d <{shape | sde | both}>]
```

Operations

describe	Lists the shapefile header and attribute column definitions (the default)
stats	Performs the describe operation and lists statistical information

Options

-d	Displays attribute column definitions	
	shape	Displays column definitions in shape format (the default)
	sde	Displays column definitions in ArcSDE format
	both	Displays column definitions in shape and ArcSDE formats
-f	Path to and name of the shapefile	
-h	Prints usage and options	
-o	Operation	
-?	Prints usage and options (use "-\?" on C shell)	

Example

```
$ shpinfo -o stats -f cities -d both
-------------------------------------
Shape File:          /world/cities
Type:                Point
Number of Shapes:    606
Extent:              minx: -165.2700042724
                     miny: -53.15000152587
                     maxx: 177.1301879882
                     maxy: 78.19999694824
Number of Nil Shapes:  0
Unverified Shapes:     0
Minimum Shape Points:  1
Maximum Shape Points:  1
Total Shape Points:    606
Average Points/Shape:  1.00
Shape Attribute Columns: 4

Name         Type   Width   Decimal Places
------------------------------------------
NAME         C      40         -
COUNTRY      C      12         -
POPULATION   N      11         -
CAPITAL      C       1         -

SDE Attribute Columns: 4

Name         Type       Width Decimal Places  NULL?
---------------------------------------------------
NAME         SE_STRING  40         -
COUNTRY      SE_STRING  12         -
POPULATION   SE_DOUBLE  12         1
CAPITAL      SE_STRING   1         -

SDE column definition string:

NAME string(40), COUNTRY string(12), POPULATION
double(12,1), CAPITAL string(1)
---------------------------------------------------
```

ArcSDE administration commands: shp2sde

This comand converts an ESRI shapefile to an ArcSDE feature class (layer). It will convert both the attributes and the geometry.

Usage syntax

```
shp2sde    -h

shp2sde    -o append -l <table,column>
           [-V <version_name>] -f <shape_file>
           [-I] [-a <{none | all |
           file=<file_name>}>]
           [-r <reject_shpfile]
           [-c <commit_interval>] [-i <service>]
           [-s <server_name>] [-D <database>]
           [-u <DB_User_name>]
           [-p <DB_User_password>] [-v]

shp2sde    -o init -l <table,column> -f
           <shape_file> [-I] [-v]
           [-a <{none | all | file=<file_name>}>]
           [-r <reject_shpfile]
           [-c <commit_interval>] [-i <service>]
           [-s <server_name>]
           [-D <database>] [-u <DB_User_name>]
           [-p <DB_User_password>]

shp2sde    -o create -l <table,column>
           [-V <version_name>] -f <shape_file>
           [-I] -g <grid_size> [{-R <SRID> |
           Spatial_Ref_Opts}]
           [-S <layer_description_str>] [-v]
           [-e <entity_mask>]
           [-k <config_keyword>] [-M <minimum_ID>]
           [-a <{none | all | file=<file_name>}>]
           [-r <reject_shpfile]
           [-c <commit_interval>] [-i <service>]
           [-s <server_name>]
           [-D <database>] [-u <DB_User_name>]
           [-p <DB_User_password>]

where Spatial_Ref_Opts is
           [-x <xoffset,yoffset,xyscale>]
           [-z <zoffset,zscale>]
```

```
[-m <moffset,mscale>]
[-G <{<projection_ID> |
file=<proj_file_name>}>]
```

Conversion table

shape	ArcSDE feature
point	ArcSDE points
multipoint	ArcSDE multipart points
arc	1:n ArcSDE lines (spaghetti) or simple lines (line strings)
	If the feature class (layer) allows both lines and simple line features, then all features that pass validation are stored as simple line features, while the rest are stored as lines. If the feature class (layer) supports only lines, then all features are stored as lines. If the feature class (layer) supports only simple line features, then all features not able to pass verification are discarded.
polygon	1:n ArcSDE area features
nil	Nil

Operations

append	Adds features to an existing layer (the default)
init	Deletes all features of an existing layer before importing new features (not allowed on versioned data)
create	Creates a new layer and imports features from the shapefile into it—an error is returned if the layer already exists

Options

-a	Attribute modes:	
	none	Does not load any attributes—the default. The business table's layer is populated with the shape records, and the spatial column is populated with a sequential number. This option allows import of data created with the "-a none" option of the sde2shp command in versions 2.1 or 2.1.1.
	all	Loads all attribute columns. If an attribute table doesn't exist for the layer, one is created. Otherwise, the incoming schema must be union compatible with the table if using the append or init option.
	file=<file_name>	File containing lines of the form <shape_column> [sde_column] The shape_column selects the column to be output, while sde_column specifies the column to load to.
-c	Commit rate (default is the AUTOCOMMIT value from giomgr.defs)	
-D	Database or data source name (not supported by all RDBMSs)	
-e	Entity types allowed (npsla3+M [{B I N IW I Q }])	

Options	(continued)
n	Nil
p	Point shapes
s	Line (spaghetti) shapes
l	Simple line (line string) shapes
a	Area shapes
3	Three-dimensional shapes can be added to the entity type mask with the "-o add" operation only.
+	Multipart shapes
M	Measures on coordinates. The [-m] option is required if measures on coordinates is a defined shape type.
B	Binary
N	Normalized coordinates
W	Well-known binary
Q	SQL type
-f	Path to and name of the shapefile
-g	Map layer class grid sizes. Grid cell sizes for levels 2 and 3 are optional. Examples are "-g 200" or "-g 200,1000,4000".
-G	Coordinate system specifier. <projection_id>—coordinate system ID (see the pedef.h file for the integer codes) file=<proj_file_name>—file containing coordinate system description string
-h	Prints usage and options
-i	ArcSDE service name

Options	(continued)
-I	Disable buffered inserts (default: ON)
-k	Layer configuration keyword. Used with the create operation only. If not specified, the default "DEFAULTS" value from the dbtune.sde file is used.
-l	Map layer table and spatial column to load. They must exist, and the user must either own the table or have INSERT access to it. If you do not own the table, qualify the table name as "owner.table".
-m	Measure offset and scale, separated by a comma (default values are 0.0, 1.0)
-M	Minimum ID. New shape IDs are assigned the larger of the minimum ID or the maximum assigned ID + one (default: 1)
-o	Operation
-p	ArcSDE user RDBMS password
-r	Rejects shapefile name for rejected shapes
-R	Spatial reference ID (SRID)
-s	ArcSDE server hostname (default: localhost)
-S	Map layer description string
-u	ArcSDE user RDBMS username
-v	Verbose option—reports records committed at the commit interval
-V	ArcSDE version name
-x	The x offset, y offset, and x,y scale values (default is 0.0, 0.0, 1.0)

Options	(continued)
-z	The z offset and scale values separated by a comma (default is 0.0, 1.0)
-?	Prints usage and options (use "-\?" in C shell)

Discussion

The shp2sde command converts shapefiles into ArcSDE feature classes (layers). This example converts a shapefile called census_data in geographic coordinates to a feature class (layer) called blocks.

```
$ shp2sde -o create -l blocks,shape -f
census_data -a all -x -200,-100,100000 -g
1,4,16 -G 4269 -e a -k block_attr -u av
```

This example converts the "world" shapefile into a feature class (layer) called "borders". The data is small scale, so the scale (in the "-x" option) is set to 10,000. The example also uses the "-r "option to write any rejected shapes to a new shapefile called rejects.

```
$ shp2sde -o create -l borders,feature -f
world -g 20,0,0 -x -180,-90,10000 -e a -k
WORLD -a all -r rejects -s stout -u world
```

ArcSDE administration commands: tbl2sde

This command converts a table format to an ArcSDE table.

Usage syntax

```
tbl2sde    -h
tbl2sde    -o append -t <table> -f <file_name>
           -T <{dBASE | INFO | SDE}> [-I]
           [-a <{all | file=<file_name>}>]
           [-c <commit_interval>]
           [-i <service>] [-s <server_name>]
           [-D <database>] -u <DB_User_name>
           [-p <DB_User_password>] [-v]
           [-w <"where_clause">]

tbl2sde    -o init -t <table> -f <file_name>
           -T <{dBASE | INFO | SDE}> [-I]
           [-a <{all | file=<file_name>}>]
           [-c <commit_interval>]
           [-i <service>] [-s <server_name>]
           [-D <database>] -u <DB_User_name>
           [-p <DB_User_password>] [-v]
           [-w <"where_clause">]

tbl2sde    -o create -t <table> -f <file_name>
           -T <{dBASE | INFO | SDE}> [-I]
           [-a <{all | file=<file_name>}>]
           [-c <commit_interval>]
           [-k <config_keyword>]
           [-w <"where_clause">] [-i <service>]
           [-s <server_name>] [-D <database>]
           -u <DB_User_name>
           [-p <DB_User_password>] [-v]
```

Operations

append	Adds records to an existing RDBMS table (the default)
init	Deletes all records of an existing RDBMS table before importing new records
create	Creates a new RDBMS table and imports records into it—an error is returned if the table already exists

Options

-a	Attribute modes:
	all Loads all columns—the default. If the table exists, the incoming schema must be union compatible with the table if using the append or init option.
	file=\<file_name\>
	File containing lines of the form \<fr_colName\> [to_colName] [type] [size] [nDecs] [NOT_NULL]
	The fr_colName selects the column to load, while the to_colName specifies the new column to load to. The allowed type, size, and nDecs (number of decimal places) values will vary according to each RDBMS.
-c	Commit rate (default is the AUTOCOMMIT value from giomgr.defs)
-D	Database or data source name—not supported by all RDBMSs
-f	Input table name—table type is defined by the -T option
-h	Prints usage and options
-i	ArcSDE service name
-I	Disable buffered inserts (default: ON)
-k	Configuration keyword from dbtune.sde file (default: DEFAULTS)
-o	Operation

Options   (continued)

-p	ArcSDE user RDBMS password
-s	ArcSDE server hostname (default: localhost)
-t	Output ArcSDE table name
-T	Input table type, either dBASE, INFO, or SDE
-u	ArcSDE user RDBMS username
-v	Verbose option—reports records committed at the commit interval
-w	SQL where clause—only used if the input table type is SDE
-?	Prints usage and options (use "-\?" in C shell)

Discussion

The tbl2sde command converts INFO and dBASE tables into ArcSDE tables. You can also use tbl2sde to selectively copy columns from an ArcSDE table into a new ArcSDE table. The example below converts a dBASE table called census_data into an ArcSDE table called block_attr.

```
$ tbl2sde -o create -t block_attr -f
census_data -T dBASE -a all -k block_attr
-u av -p mo
```

If the ArcSDE table already exists, you can add more records with the append operation. You can also remove the records from an existing table with the init operation before loading more records.

Appendix E: ArcSDE initialization parameters

The ArcSDE service initialization parameters, set in the SDEHOME\etc\giomgr.defs file, provide the functionality for the ArcSDE administrator to customize individual components of the service initialization process. The operation of and default settings for each parameter are described.

ArcSDE service initialization parameters

Parameter	Description
ATTRBUFSIZE	The size of the attribute array buffer. Defaults to 50,000.
AUTOCOMMIT	The implicit automatic commit rate within a transaction. If AUTOCOMMIT is set to 0, the transaction will commit only if the application issues an explicit commit. If it is set to a number greater than 0, the operation will commit after the number of updates specified by AUTOCOMMIT have occurred. This feature prevents transactions from becoming too large and exceeding the RDBMS logs. Defaults to 1,000.
BLOBMEM	When BLOBs are stored, the server must accumulate the BLOB chunks the application sends over the network. If the BLOB size is greater than BLOBMEM, the server writes the BLOB data to a disk file before storing it in the database. If the BLOB size is less than BLOBMEM, the server accumulates the BLOB in memory. If BLOBMEM is a negative number, the server always uses memory, regardless of the BLOB size. Defaults to 1,000,000.
CONNECTIONS	The maximum number of simultaneous connections. Defaults to 64.
LAYERS	The maximum number of feature classes. Defaults to 500.

Parameter	Description (continued)
LOCKS	The maximum number of feature class locks. Defaults to 10,000.
MAXARRAYBYTES	The maximum array bytes allocated per stream. Defaults to 550,000.
MAXARRAYSIZE	The maximum array fetch size. Defaults to 100.
MAXBLOBSIZE	The maximum size of user-defined BLOBs in bytes. Defaults to 1,000,000.
MAXBUFSIZE	The maximum buffer threshold. The minimum value is 12,288. If the MAXBUFSIZE value is greater than the minimum value but less than the MINBUFSIZE, the two values are switched. Defaults to 65,536.
MAXDISTINCT	This parameter controls the maximum number of distinct values returned by an SE_DISTINCT_STATS statistic in a call to SE_table_calculate_stats or SE_stream_calculate_table_statistics. A value of zero means an unlimited number of distinct values can be returned. Defaults to 512.

Parameter	Description (continued)	Parameter	Description (continued)
MAXINITIALFEATS	The maximum number of features allowed in the initial features argument of the sdelayer administration tool and the SE_layer_create function. This parameter prevents the inadvertent creation of excessively large initial extents for the table of a feature class. This is an ArcSDE for Oracle parameter only. Defaults to 10,000.	RASTERCOLUMNS	The maximum number of raster columns the ArcSDE instance will maintain. Defaults to 500.
		REGISTRATIONS	The maximum number of registered tables. Defaults to 1,000.
MAXSTREAMS	The maximum number of streams allowed by the server. Defaults to 8.	SHAPEPTSBUFSIZE	The size of the shape POINTS array buffer. The default value is 400,000, which is calculated for a 2-D area feature with 500 points.
MAXTABLELOCKS	The maximum number of table locks. Defaults to 10,000.	STATECACHING	Set to TRUE, the current set state for each stream is maintained in the ArcSDE server's memory. Set to FALSE, the state is re-read from disk for each stream operation. Defaults to TRUE.
MAXTIMEDIFF	Specified in seconds, the maximum time difference allowed between the server machine and a client machine. Set this parameter to -1 to disable it. Defaults to 1,800.		
MINBUFOBJECTS	The minimum number of buffer objects. Defaults to 512.	STATELOCKS	The maximum number of state locks. Defaults to 10,000.
MINBUFSIZE	The minimum buffer threshold. The minimum value is 4,096. Defaults to 16,384.	STREAMPOOLSIZE	The maximum number of allocated stream resources added to the stream pool. Until this value is exceeded, the resources of released streams are not deallocated but are added to the stream pool. The resources of the stream pool are reused whenever new streams are created. If the stream pool is full when a stream is released, its resources are deallocated. Defaults to 3.
RASTERBUFSIZE	The size of the raster buffer specified in bytes. This value must be large enough to store the largest raster tile accessed. Defaults to 102,400.		

Parameter	Description (continued)
TCPKEEPALIVE	Setting TCPKEEPALIVE to TRUE will allow the ArcSDE service to use the current system TCP/IP KEEPALIVE settings. ArcSDE servers will then be able to detect clients whose machines have crashed or have been deliberately terminated by the Windows NT Task Manager or the UNIX kill command. Be aware that if TCPKEEPALIVE is set to TRUE, a disconnection can be triggered by short-term network outages (~10 minutes). By default, TCPKEEPALIVE is set to FALSE.
TEMP	The temporary file directory. Defaults to /tmp.

Index

ArcSDE Administration Guide